"When Jesus said that he came to serve and mind the many people who help Dave Furman. This remarkable story provides soul-strengthening encouragement to those who daily bear the burdens of people like me and Dave, people who just need a helping hand, day after day. I intend to give *Being There* to the many people who are daily there for me, a quadriplegic—it's a must read for any believer who desires to follow Jesus in a life of service to others."

Joni Eareckson Tada, Founder and CEO, Joni and Friends International Disability Center

"As a long-term chronic pain sufferer, a pastor to suffering people and a friend of Dave's, I highly recommend this book. It is deeply personal, painful, and, above all, hopeful, and I am so glad he has taken the time to share his experiences. This book will point professionals, husbands, wives, and the friends of those who suffer from long-term chronic pain to the glorious truths found in the gospel of Jesus. This is not a book that offers easy solutions, but instead brings Bible-centered counsel to bear on the dark moments of life."

Mez McConnell, Senior Pastor, Niddrie Community Church, Edinburgh, Scotland; Director, 20schemes; author, *Church in Hard Places*

"As I think about the people in my world with chronic pain and ongoing difficulties, and about my awkwardness in knowing how best to walk with them, I can't imagine a better guide than Dave Furman. *Being There* is filled with insight that only someone who has walked this road can provide."

Nancy Guthrie, Bible Teacher; author, Seeing Jesus in the Old Testament Bible study series

"As we see in the Scriptures, suffering can create confusion and consternation. How are we to think rightly about darker times? Even more, how can we minister to those suffering and see them (and those nearest to them) in all their humanity to support and encourage? Dave Furman has served us well with *Being There*. It is an immensely practical book that is saturated with the truth of God's Word. I have read many books on suffering, and Dave has some unique insights that will encourage your heart. So, whether you are reading this for you, or because someone you love is currently struggling, I believe this book will serve to lift up your eyes to your loving Father who knows your situation and hasn't abandoned you!"

Matt Chandler, Lead Pastor, The Village Church, Dallas, Texas; President, Acts 29 Church Planting Network; author, *The Mingling of Souls*

"Pastors: you will love chapter 8. It will supply your church with invaluable guidelines for helping others. The rest of us: we will be better friends to those who suffer when we meditate on Dave's wise counsel."

Ed Welch, counselor and faculty, The Christian Counseling and Educational Foundation

"Too often, books are written for the hurting, and the person left out is the friend or family member who is helping the hurting. That's why Dave Furman's *Being There* will be an invaluable resource."

Deepak Reju, Associate Pastor, Capitol Hill Baptist Church, Washington, DC; President, Board of Directors, Biblical Counseling Coalition

"Dave Furman has written an insightful and needed book for those who find themselves at a loss when it comes to helping hurting people. Writing from the vantage point of one who daily struggles with pain, Dave gives authoritative counsel to those eager to learn the art of being present and the skill of giving practical care."

JR Vassar, Lead Pastor, Church at the Cross, Grapevine, Texas; author, *Glory Hunger*

"Dave Furman has written a book that will be a huge blessing to those who read it and to the suffering friends God has given them the privilege of serving. This is full of pastoral wisdom, profound theology, and deeply personal experience. It is a beautiful book with a beautiful message."

Sam Allberry, Pastor, St. Mary's Church, Maidenhead, United Kingdom; Editor, The Gospel Coalition

"So much of the Christian life is a matter of simply being there—for those who are hurting. For many years Dave Furman has faithfully modeled being there for others while he himself has benefited from those who have been there for him. This gives him a unique perspective and wisdom in crafting a book about helping the hurting. I highly recommend it."

Tim Challies, blogger, Challies.com

Being There

Being There

How to Love Those Who Are Hurting

Dave Furman

WHEATON, ILLINOIS

Library of Congress Cataloging-in-Publication Data

Names: Furman, Dave, 1979– author.
Title: Being there : how to love those who are hurting / Dave Furman.
Description: Wheaton : Crossway, 2016. | Includes bibliographical references and index.
Identifiers: LCCN 2015047227 (print) | LCCN 2016016752(ebook) | ISBN 9781433550034 (pb) |
    ISBN 9781433550041 (epub) | ISBN 9781433550065 (pdf) | ISBN 9781433550058 (mobi)
Subjects: LCSH: Consolation. | Love—Religious aspects—Christianity. | Compassion—Religious
    aspects—Christianity.
Classification: LCC BV4905.3 .F87 2016 (print) | LCC BV4905.3 (ebook) | DDC 241/.4—dc23
LC record available at https://lccn.loc.gov/2015047227

To my sweet bride, Gloria.
Thank you for trusting God in our trials and for
always pointing me to our Savior, Jesus Christ.
I love you.

Contents

Acknowledgments

My heartfelt thanks to the many who made this book possible. It was surely not an individual effort, but a community project.

My friend, John Brown, deserves the credit for the idea to write this book. You may not remember this, John, but one day in The Mill you said that a book should be written for those with hurting people in their lives. I never forgot that challenge. May this book be a blessing to both of our families and all others who have friends and family who suffer from physical pain, chronic illness, depression, and disability, and those who are suffering other kinds of losses.

I'm grateful to Tommy Nelson for teaching me to delight in God's Word and for caring for me in the midst of my own battle with depression. I often recall that time in your office when you showed compassion and care for me in my pain. You even paid out of your own pocket for me to get counseling help. Your example taught me to persevere in my trials with honesty.

John Dyer, you understood that my deepest need was to be reconciled to God through his Son, and you boldly shared your faith with me. Brother, thanks for sharing the truth with me twenty years ago, and for reminding me of that good news often.

Brady and Amber Black, you have been faithful friends for almost two decades. If you hadn't confronted me on my selfishness during our initial trials in the desert, our story would have had a bitter ending.

Ron and Kim Blough, we never would have survived our transition to live overseas if you hadn't cared for our family. Thanks for being a listening ear, a helpful hand, and lifesavers when we were in the bottom of the pit.

Elders and members of Redeemer Church of Dubai, you have loved me and my family well, and are incredibly patient with a broken and inadequate pastor. I love you so much.

Glen, Philip, Jason, Binoi, Chris, Alvin, Godly, Corsaire, Amanda, Bambie, Benjamin, and Ethan—thanks for being the most wonderful staff team a pastor could imagine!

Many thoughtful readers have helped make the book what it is through their candid advice and careful edits: Jeremy Yong, John Dyer, Eric Zeller, and Jonathan Holmes.

Anand Samuel, that day you called to encourage me about this book probably kept me from abandoning the project. Thanks for your friendship and help with this book.

A special thanks to Scott and Angela Zeller for their tireless reading of the entire manuscript and suggestions on how to improve it. This book would be a mess without your help and support.

Andrew Wolgemuth, thank you for your guidance in walking through the entire process of writing this book. I couldn't have done this without your partnership.

Tara Davis, a better editor simply does not exist!

A huge thanks also goes to the wonderful people at Crossway. The godly leadership of Lane and Ebeth Dennis is a gift to the body of Christ. To Justin Taylor, Dave DeWit, Amy Kruis, Angie Cheatham, Andrew Tebbe, Lauren Harvey, Matt Tully, Clair Kassebaum, Josh Dennis, and Claire Cook, thanks for believing in this project and for your encouragement.

Aliza, Norah, Judson, and Troy, you have been patient with your dad as we've struggled through our trials together. Thanks for your love and care as you button my shirts for me, open doors, and untie my shoelaces after I work out.

Gloria, you've been a constant support through it all. Through the darkest moments you were faithful to God and to the vows you made years ago. Thanks for modeling Christ for me, for our children, and for all those around us. I love you, sweetheart.

Introduction

I keep a photograph in my office of me picking up my fiancée, Gloria, in my strong, capable arms. A few months later on our honeymoon, we were white-knuckling the handles of a raft in the rapids of Costa Rica. Fast forward a decade and our circumstances were quite different. On our tenth anniversary, a kind stranger offered me his help as he saw Gloria trying her best to lift my disabled body out of an inner tube at a water park. I can only imagine what was going through that gentleman's mind when he saw me struggling to float down the lazy river.

When I was a child, I played tennis and earned two black belts in karate. As a university student, I played pick-up football on my college campus. I never dreamed that I would soon have a physical disability. It's been over ten years now since my doctor discovered that the nerves in my arms weren't working properly—firing off chronic pain signals to my brain and twisting themselves into painful neuromas. I've had four major surgeries on my arms, gone through over a dozen invasive procedures in the hospital, worked for hundreds of hours in therapy, and taken a cocktail of medicines and homeopathic remedies to give me some relief. But nothing has really worked.

I never thought that there would be times when I couldn't lift a cup of water to my lips to take a drink or would need the help of my preschool-aged daughter to button my shirt. I can count on one hand the number of times I've been able to hold any one of my four babies. After my wife makes sure that all of our children are buckled in properly to their car seats, she comes around to the passenger side of the minivan and opens my door. Once she is in the driver's seat, she leans over to buckle my seat belt for me.

On a trip to the United States for a conference, I was eating lunch with a big group of pastors. Without a word, Mack, one of the elders of our church, leaned over and graciously cut my steak for me so I could eat it. Sensing the awkwardness around the table of pastors who were not aware of my disability, he joked, "Don't your elders serve *you* like this?"

Eight years ago, our family moved overseas to plant churches on the Arabian Peninsula. I had surgery a few months prior and was recovering very well. We were hopeful that the pain and disability were now behind us. Then one night while driving in a parking lot as Gloria did some late-night shopping, I felt a sharp burning pain in both of my arms. The problem was back, and it was back with a vengeance. We were so excited about what we had perceived as total healing and were thrilled about plans for the new churches we'd be planting, but instead our hopes went spiraling downward.

The next week a rash of painful bumps covered both of my hands down to my fingertips, and I couldn't bear to touch anything. Depression engulfed me, and I would stay awake most nights pacing back and forth in my bedroom on the verge of losing my mind. In those dark hours of the night Gloria thought I was going crazy and took comfort in the fact that I was not physically able to get out of the house and wander into the desert. We had tried everything, and nothing worked. There was no relief, no joy.

This is how our ministry started in the Middle East. Every weekend Gloria would buckle our baby daughter and me into our seats, and she'd drive us two hours to Dubai to meet people, attend our partner church, and build contacts for a potential church plant in the center of that city. I would "turn it on" for a few hours, be cordial, cast vision for the church, and then I'd become a shell of myself for the next five days. I was just trying to survive.

And even worse, I had turned into a grumpy, passive-aggressive man. To my great regret, I had completely disengaged from my daughter. I not-so-secretly blamed Gloria for everything. If I was in pain, it was her fault. I didn't know I was struggling with depression at the time, but I knew something wasn't right and I wanted to snap out of it—but nothing changed. The darkness simply would not lift. I was disabled, depressed, and angry.

Throughout this trial I felt like the victim and the only one who was suffering. Nobody understood how I felt. The whole world revolved around me and existed to serve me and help me. I started playing the "if only" game. It's the game where in your mind you say, "If only _____, then I'll be happy." For example:

When I'm hungry: If only I had something to eat, *then* I would have joy.

When people criticize me: If only they would go away, *then* I would be happy.

If my bank account is empty: If only I had more money, *then* I could give my kids the life they deserve.

If only my family member hadn't died...

If only I didn't have this health condition...

If only... if only...

For me, the "if only" game was all about having healthy arms. If only my arms weren't hurting, *then* I'd be happy. I said this every day, maybe even every hour, to myself. It became my gospel. John Calvin famously said that our hearts are idol factories, and we are constantly creating different idols to bring us happiness.[1] For me it was the idol of comfort that I thought would come only if I had healthy arms and no more pain.

I didn't realize how much my idol pursuit was affecting my wife. I wasn't alone in my distress as I paced the floor those long nights in our bedroom. Gloria was awake too. She was praying for me and was also struggling to hold fast to her hope in God. While I was pacing the floors wondering if I'd ever be able to hold my baby, my wife paced in her own mind wondering if she would ever have a "normal" husband. My idol was the comfort of healthy arms; Gloria's idol was the comfort of a husband with healthy arms. Now, on the other side of that season of depression, I can see clearly that pain and suffering affect not only the one directly experiencing them, but also *everyone* around that person.

Unfortunately our story is not a unique or isolated tale. I've talked to many families that have been affected by chronic pain, disability, sickness, loss, and depression. A fellow pastor and friend of mine named John also struggles with a disability in both of his hands. He has a hard time typing and doing normal household chores, which leaves his wife to pick up the slack and wait patiently for times when he feels well enough to contribute. John encouraged me to write this book for those caring for the hurting. I am writing out of my experience of being helped in incredible ways by others in my disability. There are much better books on the topic of suffering. However, this is not another book about suffering for the one who suffers. It's a book for everyone who knows people who suffer from pain and loss and wants to see the Rock of Ages underneath their feet. I think it's safe to say that this is a book for all of us.

The aim of chapter 1 is to bring encouragement and healing for you, the caregiver who suffers in silence. Before I can even talk about how to help those who are hurting, you need to first examine your own heart in the process. You can't pretend that you haven't experienced loss and grief in another's pain. The goal of chapter 2 is to show where your strength in helping the hurting comes from. The remaining chapters will help you practically care for those hurting in your life. There's even an afterword written by my wife, Gloria, where she honestly shares her experience in caring for me in the darkest times.

We all know people who are in pain. We may have a child who who struggles with a learning disability, a spouse who is disabled, a friend fighting cancer, a neighbor or fellow church member with chronic pain, an aging parent suffering with any number of illnesses, or those who have lost loved ones.

Maybe you have found yourself asking the following questions:

- How should I, as a church member, respond when a fellow church member is hurting?
- How do I, as a husband or wife, serve and love my spouse who struggles with chronic pain and is distant and emotionally unengaged?
- How should I care for my aging parents in a way that honors both them and God?
- What truth should I speak into the life of a friend who is on his deathbed?
- How do I interact with my cousin who is paralyzed and is living in despair?
- How do I care for a wife who is brokenhearted over a marriage that seems to be falling apart?
- How do I encourage young married couples who are struggling with miscarriages or infertility?

Maybe you're struggling in your care, and you feel like you can't go on and there is nothing you can do to help the hurting person in your life. You're right, on your own you can't. The goal of this entire book is to point you to Jesus, who is your only hope, and to walk you through some ways you can love those who hurt with the strength God provides.

1

Grieving Your Loss in
Another's Pain

Even though my pain is not the most apparent (I wear no casts or braces), it is relatively easy to spot. I can't use my arms normally, and so I have a loss of physical capabilities. I have to ask for plasticware at restaurants when their forks are too heavy for me to use. I am reminded every day that I'm not strong enough to pick up my children. I ask my six-year old daughter, Norah, to untie my shoes after I come back from exercising. Though my loss is easy to see, what about the loss my wife has experienced? It's often overlooked, but she's lost much through this trial as well. Unlike most other wives, she doesn't have a husband who can physically help her around the house. I can't take out the trash, move the furniture, pick up a wet towel from the bathroom floor, or make the bed. She recently handled a particularly messy potty training accident and joked that it might be the mess that tops all messes. She would know, since she has changed virtually every diaper for our four children. My wife not only doesn't have the physical help she needs from me, but she has to spend *additional* time helping me.

She also experiences the emotional and mental anguish that accompanies this type of loss. For example, after leaving the Opryland Hotel in Nashville once after a quick stay, Gloria opened my car door, helped buckle my seatbelt, and managed to move the big cart with all of our suitcases to the back of the vehicle. She loaded each bag into the trunk and then closed it up. Three women sitting on a nearby bench had been watching this scene play out. One woman called out to Gloria and told her that it's not right that her "good-for-nothing husband" just sat there and made her do all the work. My gentle and patient wife calmly replied that her husband was disabled, and then she got in the car before any tears arrived. Stuff like this happens all the time. We don't often walk through airport security together because we're tired of getting barked at by officials because I am not helping put the shoes, bags, laptops, car seats, and stroller onto the X-ray belt for screening.

You probably have your own scenes you've lived through—scenes where you think that if only people knew what was *really* going on, they might cut you some slack and help you. Anticipating and dealing with this kind of social anxiety can be quite distressing for a caretaker. As you care for and love the sufferer, there's a different kind of suffering that you experience that is often left unaddressed. If you are caring for someone who's hurting, then the first step you need to take is to honestly grieve the loss that *you* suffer. This first chapter will address how you come to terms with your own loss in someone else's pain.

Grieving Your Loss

If you're helping someone who is hurting, you have given up something to care for them. You have lost something yourself in the process. I lost the health of my arms, but my wife lost a husband with healthy arms. Caregivers face the temptation to believe the lie that their spouse or friend has nothing to contribute. They battle the exhaustion of constantly defending the ones they care for or worrying about people thinking ill of them. My children also deal with the loss of not having a dad who can do things like pick them up, stop them from tumbling while on their roller skates, or open a box of crackers. They have to learn patience with me, and they can become frustrated when I'm unable to do something that their mom could do for them.

My church staff, who frequently have to stop what they're doing to help me or to give of their personal time to help our family, also experiences loss. For example, Chris has been exceptional at caring for me and my family regarding our physical needs. Whether it's helping to get our car fixed or giving me a ride somewhere, he's always available, and there is a cost for him in my disability. He's happy to help, but it's certainly a different dynamic than having a pastor who is healthy enough to take care of himself and physically help others. You might find yourself in any number of difficult situations.

The one who loses a family member to cancer experiences deep pain and sorrow from the loss. So does the middle-aged teacher who takes repeated trips across the country to care for his aging father who is struggling with Alzheimer's and can hardly remember who his own son is anymore. A young mother spends most of her day trying to fight for joy as she cares for her disabled daughter and her house. A friend doesn't know what to say anymore after igniting the anger of her depressed best friend for the one hundredth time.

My point is that while we are all, by God's grace, privy to extraordinary gifts from his hands through these trials (like learning patience, etc.), we must acknowledge the pain of loss with our eyes wide open. Maybe you've thought that as a Christian you have to smile and pretend to be okay when someone asks you how you are doing. Perhaps you think that if you're grieving, then you're dishonoring God. This isn't so.

While an incredible preacher in London, Charles Spurgeon often battled depression and massive despair. On one occasion he was out of ministry for six months and had to leave the country. He was so depressed he had difficulty getting out of bed. He said that when depression would come upon him, he felt like a man who was fighting the mist; it was everywhere, and he couldn't hit it.[1]

In some ways, our grief as Christians is amplified because our hearts of stone have been made hearts of flesh, and now we hurt for other people differently. You hurt for your family and friends who are suffering. It's imperative that you are honest about the pain that you are going through. Rather than just trying harder and keeping it to yourself, it's important that you grieve your loss and come to terms with your reality.

Jerry Sittser writes,

> The pain of loss is unrelenting. It stalks and chases until it catches us. It is as persistent as wind on the prairies, as constant as cold in the Antarctic, as erosive as a spring flood. It will not be denied and there is no escape from it. In the end denial, bargaining, binges, and anger are mere attempts to deflect what will eventually conquer us all. Pain will have its day because loss is undeniably, devastatingly real.[2]

Because of the realness of loss, the direction of your life has changed. The way you live and rest and work and go about your life is different now.

Grief is work, and sometimes it's very hard work. It can be overwhelming. H. Norman Wright, in his excellent book *Experiencing Grief*, says, "Grief is like the visitor who has overstayed his welcome."[3] Grieving is a messy process, and you yearn for it to just go away. You don't know when a sunset or a trip to the pharmacy is going to trigger a memory that crushes your spirit. Sometimes even a moment of quiet will lead your mind to wandering to emotions you can't control. Grief comes and goes, and there is no way to schedule it in your day planner.

After my pain came back upon our move to the Arabian Peninsula, my friend John and I had a memorable phone conversation. John mentioned the story of King David mourning for thirty days after his child died. We both chuckled at the thought of someone taking thirty days to cry, wail, and mourn their loss publicly. It sounds ridiculous in today's society, but there was probably something very healthy about it. We still suffer today and mourn our losses, but we're often made to feel like we need to choke down our tears and grief instead of dealing with it in healthy and honest ways.

We all grieve and process loss in different ways, but it's essential that you don't stay in denial. You must make it known that it's difficult, that you're struggling. Many professional counselors have said that the single most vital component in healing from pain and loss is having the support of other people. It's important to share with others that you're grieving and going through difficulty. Don't walk this journey alone.

I wonder if this idea of personal grieving is new to you. Perhaps the idea of grieving your loss is uncomfortable and unknown. Maybe you're not sure what's entailed, why you ought to recognize your grief, or where you should start in grieving your loss in someone else's pain. In the rest of this chapter, I'll explain two ways you can do that.

Weeping Honestly

Often in the church Christians are taught that weeping is failing to trust God. There is seldom a place for sorrow and lamentation among Christians—no freedom to cry out to the Lord. However, the book of Psalms is filled with what are called psalms of lament. At least two of them show the psalmist crying out to the Lord without even a hint of hope intertwined with his grief.[4]

Psalm 88 is one of these psalms:

O LORD, God of my salvation;
    I cry out day and night before you.
Let my prayer come before you;
    incline your ear to my cry!
For my soul is full of troubles,
    and my life draws near to Sheol.
I am counted among those who go down to the pit;
    I am a man who has no strength,
like one set loose among the dead,
    like the slain that lie in the grave,
like those whom you remember no more,
    for they are cut off from your hand.
You have put me in the depths of the pit,
    in the regions dark and deep.
Your wrath lies heavy upon me,
    and you overwhelm me with all your waves. *Selah*
You have caused my companions to shun me;
    you have made me a horror to them.
I am shut in so that I cannot escape;
    my eye grows dim through sorrow.
Every day I call upon you, O LORD;
    I spread out my hands to you.
Do you work wonders for the dead?
    Do the departed rise up to praise you? *Selah*
Is your steadfast love declared in the grave,
    or your faithfulness in Abaddon?
Are your wonders known in the darkness,
    or your righteousness in the land of forgetfulness?
But I, O LORD, cry to you;
    in the morning my prayer comes before you.

O Lord, why do you cast my soul away?
    Why do you hide your face from me?
Afflicted and close to death from my youth up,
    I suffer your terrors; I am helpless.
Your wrath has swept over me;
    your dreadful assaults destroy me.
They surround me like a flood all day long;
    they close in on me together.
You have caused my beloved and my friend to shun me;
    my companions have become darkness.

This is a dark psalm. Biblical scholar Derek Kidner says, "There is no sadder prayer in the Psalter."[5] The psalmist, Heman, is clearly depressed and is hardly even fighting for hope. Psalm 88 shows that believers can be in darkness, and it's possible to pray and not see any relief. The psalmist is certainly praying, as you can see in verses 1, 9, and 13, but God doesn't seem to be giving him the help he needs. He feels that God is distant from him. And not only does he not see any help coming from God, he sees God as the source of his pain. He feels God's wrath upon him as he sits in the dark pit. Even his former companions have now turned against him. He's not being especially reverent nor is he being mushy and letting God know that he loves him. By the end of the psalm, he starts asking the "why" questions. All he can see as he looks back on his life is his affliction and suffering.

What, then, is the purpose of this psalm? Kidner helpfully identifies three key lessons from the psalm. The first is that it is possible that a believer will endure unrelieved suffering in this earthly life. The joyful ending of most psalms is a bonus and not a guarantee. The withholding of relief is not proof of God's displeasure or defeat. The second lesson is that our pain and suffering are not the final word in our lives. They are reminders to us that we wait for the redemption of our bodies on the last day. The third lesson is that this author, like Job, does not give up. The darkness will not lift, but the author still prays.[6]

The psalm shows that believers can be overcome by darkness for long periods of time. They can attend church services, pray prayers, and be in fellowship, and yet find no improvement. Things don't always work themselves out quickly in the believer's life, but God is there. Tim Keller, in his excellent book, *Walking with God in Pain and Suffering*, notes that prayers like Heman's in Psalm 88 are an encouragement to us because they show that God didn't censor the prayers in Scripture. Christians do at times pray like the psalmist. Sometimes we are weak and falling apart. It's in moments of despair when all has been lost that we can learn to depend on God and not on other things. But we must, like the psalmist, be honest about our suffering with ourselves and others.[7]

Finding Hope in the Loss

We need to weep honestly at the loss we've experienced, but it's a weeping that is fundamentally grounded in hope. A second way we deal with our grief is to find hope in our loss.

Psalm 51:17 says, "The sacrifices of God are a broken spirit; a broken and contrite heart, O God, you will not despise."

God will not despise a broken heart. David's life seems to illustrate this point. He went through so much pain that at the end of Psalm 39 he utters a prayer of desperation. David actually prays that the Lord would look away from him. In his desperation, he can see no other ending than death, and he tells God to just leave him alone.

David says,

> Hear my prayer, O LORD,
> and give ear to my cry;
> hold not your peace at my tears!
> For I am a sojourner with you,

a guest, like all my fathers.
Look away from me, that I may smile again,
before I depart and am no more! (Ps. 39:12–13)

The truth is, God does not look away from his people. However, David's prayer reminds us of a unique time when God did look away from someone. Keller points out that the only person who sought God and truly did lose God's face and did experience total darkness was Jesus. He really was forsaken by God. At the moment he died, everyone had betrayed, denied, rejected, or forsaken him, even his Father. Total darkness was indeed Jesus's only friend.[8] Keller says, "It was Jesus who truly experienced the ultimate darkness—the cosmic rejection we deserved so that we can know the Lord will never leave or forsake us."[9] Jesus experienced this forsaking on the cross: "Now from the sixth hour there was darkness over all the land until the ninth hour. And about the ninth hour Jesus cried out with a loud voice, saying, 'Eli, Eli, lema sabachthani?' that is, 'My God, my God, why have you forsaken me?'" (Matt. 27:45–46). But even in the midst of his rejection, Jesus remained hopeful in the will of God. Even facing his death, Jesus could say in John 17:5, "And now, Father, glorify me in your own presence with the glory that I had with you before the world existed." Jesus rested in the plan that the triune God has set forth in the beginning—to glorify himself and save sinners by Christ's death on the cross. The abandonment Jesus experienced on the cross really is good news to us. Because Jesus was truly abandoned by God the Father, we will never be abandoned by God.[10]

Compassionate caretaker, do you think he will abandon you now in the midst of your own genuine loss? *No,* he won't. Rest assured that because of Jesus, there is always hope, even in the darkest moments of your life. Jesus faced the cross and said, "My God, my God, why have you forsaken me?" so that you would never be forsaken (Matt. 27:46). Jesus is now your high priest who has gone through what you've gone through, and he did it to bring you to God. Jesus, in his death on the cross, shows his people the ultimate display of love. If Jesus went to the cross for you, he'll certainly be with you in your very real pain. Meditate on the following verses and let the promises of God encourage you and comfort your heart.

Blessed are those who mourn, for they shall be comforted. (Matt. 5:4)

Blessed be the God and Father of our Lord Jesus Christ, the Father of mercies and God of all comfort, who comforts us in all our affliction, so that we may be able to comfort those who are in any affliction, with the comfort with which we ourselves are comforted by God. (2 Cor. 1:3–4)

Truly, truly, I say to you, you will weep and lament, but the world will rejoice. You will be sorrowful, but your sorrow will turn into joy. When a woman is giving birth, she has sorrow because her hour has come, but when she has delivered the baby, she no longer remembers the anguish, for joy that a human being has been born into the world. So also you have sorrow now, but I will see you again, and your hearts will rejoice, and no one will take your joy from you. (John 16:20–22)

Furthermore, Psalm 88 was meant to be read within the entire Psalter, which is filled with grace-driven hope.

God is our refuge and strength,
    a very present help in trouble.
Therefore we will not fear though the earth gives way,
    though the mountains be moved into the heart of the sea.
        (Ps. 46:1–2)

I lift up my eyes to the hills.
    From where does my help come?

My help comes from the LORD,
> who made heaven and earth.
He will not let your foot be moved;
> he who keeps you will not slumber.
Behold, he who keeps Israel
> will neither slumber nor sleep. (Ps. 121:1–4)

The LORD is my shepherd; I shall not want.
> He makes me lie down in green pastures.
He leads me beside still waters.
> He restores my soul.
He leads me in paths of righteousness
> for his name's sake.
Even though I walk through the valley of the shadow of death,
> I will fear no evil,
for you are with me;
> your rod and your staff,
> they comfort me.
You prepare a table before me
> in the presence of my enemies;
you anoint my head with oil;
> my cup overflows.
Surely goodness and mercy shall follow me
> all the days of my life,
and I shall dwell in the house of the LORD forever. (Psalm 23)

It's interesting that in Psalm 88, the psalmist offers no hope in the content of the psalm, and yet the author's name and job are listed in the title of the psalm. This man's life, ministry, and suffering were no accidents or errors in God's plan, but his divine hand was behind everything. If there's hope in the psalm, it's in the title: "O LORD, God of my salvation." Of the title line of the psalm, Kidner says, "Burdened and despondent as he was, his existence was far from pointless. If it was a living death, in God's hands it was to bear much fruit."[11]

God will not abandon you in your grief and pain in helping the hurting. Your life of service to the depressed, disabled, or wounded may be exhausting and even painful for your own heart. You may be a silent sufferer, but God hears your cries for help and he sees your every minute of sacrificial service. You need to come to him with honesty, expectant that he will be with you in the midst of it. There is hope for the hopeless.

2

Walking with God

Years ago, Gloria and I embarked on an epic road trip around the United States. We were heading from the South to New Hampshire, so that I could take part in a pastoral internship in the center of "moose country." On our road trip, we stopped to visit with an organization doing ministry overseas and were able to meet with the leaders.

We had lunch with the president for what we thought would be merely an informative time, but it ended up being one of the most impacting conversations we've ever had. The lunch started innocently enough with him and his wife at a neighborhood Mexican restaurant (I don't think I've ever had a bad meeting over Mexican food!). I'll never forget Steve's answer to what I thought was a simple question. I asked him, "What's your hope for the ministers in your ministry?" His answer was profound and rather unexpected. He said that his priority for those in his organization wasn't to see how big their churches could become, how many converts they won to Christ, how much money they were able to raise, or even how long they stayed in the ministry. He said the only goal and measure of success he had for the workers who were part of the ministry is that they would love God more when they left the organization than when they started. I think I just about dropped my tortilla chip in the salsa bowl. To hear Steve say that he was hoping for increased love for the Lord floored me. He looked me in the eye and said, "When you go overseas, the goal for the end of your ministry is that you should be able to say this: Do you love God more today than when you first stepped foot on the sand of the Arabian Peninsula?"

Steve's point in telling us this was that if we don't first love God, we won't have any strength for ministry. One flows directly out of the other. Wow! For someone as driven as I am, I am always enamored by results and getting more and more. And here was the president of this organization telling me that in one sense, that wouldn't define our success overseas. Success could only be had by diving into the correct source for our strength in the first place. Our goal in loving the hurting should be to first love our God.

Steve's words echoed those of Jesus: "For what does it profit a man to gain the whole world and forfeit his soul?" (Mark 8:36). What Steve was trying to tell me was to get my priorities straight. If all you ever try to do is get results, then you will fail, because in your own strength you can't bring about spiritual fruit. Steve's point was that if you're not walking with God, then you will not have the strength to serve God.

As we consider our topic of loving the hurting, this especially rings true. Are you investing in your relationship with God? Are you walking with him? If not, then you will have no strength to help the hurting. Pretty soon all your work will be in your own strength, and eventually you will break down. You could ask Steve's question of yourself as you help those who are hurting. Have I drawn closer to God as I help my friend? Are my affections for Christ higher now than they were before the trial began? The aim of this chapter is to encourage you to walk with God as you help the hurting. If you are not walking with God, then you will have nothing substantial to help your friend in their pain.

A New and Greater Affection

In his famous sermon, "The Expulsive Power of a New Affection," Scottish minister Thomas Chalmers said no one ever changed a habit just by trying. You can't fight sin, like anger or bitterness, just by girding up your loins and saying, "I don't want to feel that way." Trying harder won't be enough to root out those feelings. Chalmers writes: "The heart is so constituted that the only way to dispossess it of an old affection is by the expulsive power of a new one. What you need to drive out an old passion is a new passion, a greater passion. What you need is an over-mastering positive passion."[1]

If you don't have the strength to love the hurting, trying harder is not the trick. You need Jesus. Jesus is better than anything our hearts could possibly attach themselves to. Since we've been given new hearts through faith in Christ's death and resurrection, what do we have to do with lesser hopes?

We must remember to love those who are hurting not because they've done anything for us, but because of what Jesus has already done for us. You will get the strength to help the hurting only when you understand what God has done for you in the gospel. The gospel message begins with creation. We were all created by God to be in perfect relationship with him. Humans were the apex of his creation. Far greater than the mountains or the seas, at the very center of God's creation are you and I. He made mankind in his image. In some miraculous way, we humans uniquely reveal something about God. And we were created to enjoy God, to be in a loving relationship with our Lord. But things went wildly wrong when the first two humans, Adam and Eve, saw God but also saw an opportunity to be their own gods. They didn't want to live under God's loving rule and reign and chose to rebel against God. It is this sin that all of us are born into and follow every day of our lives. On our own we want to have nothing to do with God.

We've all rejected and rebelled against our Creator, Maker, and God. It's not like burning the food you were cooking for dinner. Or hurting the feelings of a friend. Our sin involves the *created* rejecting the perfect *Creator*. And so we all deserve death and judgment. This is the only punishment that fits the crime. We've offended an infinitely holy God. The punishment must then be of infinite measure. This is the just judgment that hangs over every one of us apart from divine intervention.

In fact, Paul says in the book of Ephesians that we are already dead in our trespasses and sins. He uses the imagery of a dead corpse. According to legend, when nineteenth-century Texan leader Sam Houston was baptized, the minister told him, "Your sins are washed away." And Houston replied, "God help the fish." Now, of course, his sins weren't floating downstream, because they were placed on Christ at the cross, but what he was saying (rather humorously) is that he understood that he was a wicked man. Apart from God's intervention in this man's life and in our lives, we are dead and without hope. That's the plight of the sinner. Our sin separates us from God. We can't create a remedy for our sin—no good work can erase our bad works and sin nature. There is no hope apart from God.

But thankfully, God himself *gives* us hope. God in his grace provided a way of reconciliation through the death and resurrection of the Son of God. For you, the Christian, he left the glories of heaven and was born of a virgin in an insignificant town. But he wasn't an ordinary baby; this child was born for the express purpose of dying. Jesus lived to die. He willingly set his face toward Jerusalem, because he knew that it was there that he would be lifted up on the cross, taking upon himself the sins of his people as an atoning sacrifice. He faced God's wrath for us and died in the place of sinners as our substitute. Christ was punished for our sin and killed in our place.

Jesus's lifeless body was taken down from the cross and placed in a tomb. But then what happened? The cords of death could not hold him. He was raised by God to resurrection life, triumphing over death. On the third day the tomb was empty. Hundreds of witnesses saw the risen Christ. Jesus's sacrifice for your sin was accepted by his Father. As a Christian it should shock you that God saved you. You were dead, *but* now you're alive. It's an amazing love that our God should die for us! That's a truth that should never cease to amaze us.

The apostle Paul in 1 Timothy 1:14 writes, "And the grace of our Lord overflowed for me with the faith and love that are in Christ Jesus." It's a love that never ends. I read a story of an artist who once submitted a painting of Niagara Falls to an art show but forgot to give it a title. The gallery came up with its own title, "More to Follow."[2] Niagara Falls has been flooding the areas below for thousands of years with life-giving water. This is a beautiful picture of the grace of God—there is always more grace he is pouring out. God is a never-ending conduit of grace for his people.

Because of God's unconditional love for us, we can go forward and offer unconditional love to others. Even in the difficult times, as believers we are armed with the Spirit of God, reminded of the promises of God, and encouraged by the love of God. We must not react to our friends' negative responses to us, but instead, act in light of Christ's forgiving response to our sin. The fact that Jesus saves you through his death and resurrection affects the way you wake up in the morning and serve your friends again and again.

The gospel is true and trustworthy, and it must affect our lives. The good news of God's saving grace in the gospel never gets old. And realizing we don't deserve it always leads us to worship. That's why we don't move on to a better message. There is no better news.

The good news of the gospel is balm for our weary souls every day. Just like when I get home and my kids run and give me the same hugs they did the day before. And I see my wife, and I tell her that I love her. She knows I love her, but I still tell her again and again. It's old news—she knows it—but it's sweet to hear over again. Walking with God starts with a renewed understanding of the gospel, which infiltrates our hearts. In order to adequately care for others, we first need this news (and the Spirit of God) to stir in us a new and greater affection.

Communion with God

I once heard a pastor contrast sticking a piece of wood in the ground with planting a tree. Both are in a similar physical position, but their condition couldn't be more different. Through its roots, the tree is reaching out into the soil in which it lives and is drawing from it the life-giving nutrients that support its life. In John 15:4 Jesus says, "Abide in me, and I in you. As the branch cannot bear fruit by itself, unless it abides in the vine, neither can you, unless you abide in me." When that which is abiding draws from that which supports it, its life is sustained. Similarly, unless we are abiding in Christ, we cannot be effective at loving others. Your strength to care for the hurting comes directly from Christ. You have no hope to truly help the hurting if you are disconnected from Christ, the vine. The secret of bearing spiritual fruit is not in reading this book, being more disciplined with your time, or drinking more coffee. Those things may help (my wife loves her coffee!), but there is no substitute for a relationship with Christ. Abide in him. There has to be a living connection between the branch and the source of life, Jesus. Apart from that vital, living relationship, there is nothing we can do.

I use a copy of an old book written in the nineteenth century called *Words to Winners of Souls* as my mouse pad. It was written by the great Scottish Presbyterian, Horatius Bonar, and it has marked my life. It has so impacted me that I have all of our pastoral interns read it as one of the first books of their internship. In one of our first meetings of the year, I read the following excerpt aloud to them:

> We have allowed business, study, or active labor to interfere with our closet hours. . . . Why so many meetings with our fellow men, yet so few meetings with God? Why so little being alone, so little thirsting of the soul for the sweet calm, sweet hours of unbroken solitude, when God and His child hold fellowship together as if they could never part? It is the want of these solitary hours that not only injures our own growth in grace but makes us such unprofitable members of the church of Christ, and that renders our lives useless. In order to grow in grace, we must be much alone. . . . And so it is also only in this way that we become truly useful to others. It is when coming out fresh from communion with God that we go forth to do His work successfully. It is in the closet that we get our vessels so filled with blessing, that, when we come forth, we cannot contain it to ourselves but must, as by a blessed necessity, pour it out whithersoever we go. . . . Nearness to God, fellowship with God, waiting upon God, resting in God, have been too little the characteristics either of our private or our ministerial walk. Hence our example has been so powerless, our labors so unsuccessful, our sermons so meager, our whole ministry so fruitless and feeble.[3]

I'm terrified when I read those words. They really just say the same thing that Jesus says in John 15 (that apart from Christ we can do nothing), and they serve as a warning and exhortation toward those caring for the hurting. Usually you don't get warnings as a caretaker, do you? But here we have a warning: If you are not abiding in Christ, then your ministry is empty and useless. You are like a dry sponge without an ounce of hope to squeeze out to another. You have to walk with God in order to help those who are hurting walk closer with God.

This will be a challenge for you if you find it hard to get time alone. Perhaps your caregiving requires you to constantly be in the presence of one who is hurting. Or maybe you are a mother of young children and you hardly have a minute of quiet time. Many lives are characterized by being in the company of others and do not have the luxury of being alone. Just think of all the believers in parts of the world where they live together in small homes with their extended family members. There are no soft armchairs in the corner with a side table for your coffee-accompanied quiet time. Even so, I think Bonar's principle and Christ's exhortation still apply. You must be much with Christ before you are anything for anybody else. Even in the chaos of life, you should, like a deer pants for water, strive for moments of communion with our great God in the middle of it all.

Heart Work Is Hard Work

It is easier for most of us to check off things on our to-do list than it is to commune with God. Even as we are spending time with God, it seems most difficult to examine our hearts and ask God to transform us. Heart work is indeed hard work. But it's a most necessary work that God does in your heart as you care for the hurting. Seventeenth-century English Puritan John Flavel says it's the most difficult, constant, and important work in the believer's life. He writes,

> To repress the outward acts of sin, and compose the external part of thy life in a laudable manner, is no great matter; even carnal persons, by the force of common principles, can do this: but to kill the root of corruption within, to set and keep a holy government over thy thoughts, to have all things lie straight and orderly in the heart, this is not easy. It is a constant work.

The keeping of the heart is a work that is never done until life is ended. There is no time or condition in the life of a Christian which will suffer an intermission of this work.[4]

If you're going to help the hurting, your heart needs to be healthy. Your efforts in your own strength can go on for only so long.

So what should you do? I don't have anything new or inventive to say; I can only repeat that which we tell every new believer. We do not survive on bread alone, but we must devour God's Word. It may seem like doing anything is a massive burden when times are tough and there seems to be no way out. But what thrills the heart is filling the mind with the ways the Trinitarian God is pursuing us. Jesus demonstrated this love by first loving God with all his heart and soul and then overflowing with ever-ready love for others. This sacrificial love was modeled for us during his earthly life and then climactically portrayed in his death on the cross. If we remember God's love for us, our response will be to fill our hearts and minds with truths rather than simply feeling burdened by a laundry list of spiritual disciplines.

We need to fill our hearts and minds by meditating on God's Word day and night (Josh. 1:8). Oftentimes when we think of meditation, we think of some kind of Eastern meditation, a kind of emptying of the mind, trying to rid ourselves of conscious thoughts. Sometimes so-called "Christian" books pass off this kind of meditation on nothing as truly free spiritual worship. This is actually the opposite of biblical meditation. In biblical meditation, we fill our minds with God's truth. We pick up those things God has said in his Word and we put them in our minds, and that's what we focus on.

Deuteronomy 17:18–20 give us a beautiful picture of this. Here we learn that the first task for a new king was to write on a scroll, word for word, his own copy of God's law. His first task was not to appoint his royal officials or redecorate the palace, but to copy huge portions of Scripture by hand. This would then become his personal copy that he would read for the rest of his life. He was to go through it slowly so that it would be on his heart.

We are to saturate ourselves in God's Word. This is the primary way God speaks and reveals himself to us today. But sadly, we often look elsewhere for hope and direction. We need reminders to look to God. Here are a few questions that you can answer to see where you are getting strength in your pursuit of the hurting:

- Are you reading God's Word regularly? This is not about earning God's favor by checking a box to prove you've had seven devotional times this week. It's so you don't forget God's promises for yourself or for those who are hurting. If you want a word from God, study God's Word.
- Are you hiding God's Word in your heart? Perhaps you can start by memorizing gospel-saturated passages like Romans 8:31–34 or 1 Corinthians 15:3–4. Or even better, you may stop and meditate on Scripture. We recently held a seminary class in Dubai where Dr. Bruce Ware assigned Scripture meditation. Rather than simply memorizing Scripture, he wanted us to think about it, ponder it, read it over and over again, pray through it, apply it to our lives, and talk to others about it. Scripture meditation is a great way to exercise our souls. It's an opportunity for us to examine our lives in light of God's Word. A great end result is that if you spend enough time meditating on it, you will probably have it memorized.
- Are you praying through Scripture? Are you opening up God's Word to read it and pray through those truths?
- Are you fasting and asking God for strength to help the hurting? Christians do this not for the sake of penance or weight loss, but for the purpose of spiritual gain. We refrain from eating for a period of time to concentrate on pursuing Christ. A fast may be for one meal or a whole day or even several days. You take the time you would be eating to pray

and read God's Word. It's an opportunity to consider any un-repentant sin and to pray for guidance and strength in your service. The constant hunger pangs remind you that God is your all-sufficient Savior.

- Are you in a small group where you're studying the Bible with others? Do you get together with a friend to read the Bible together?
- Are you maximizing your commute by listening to an audio Bible or Christ-centered sermons?
- Are you a member of a gospel-proclaiming church where you can sit under the regular preaching of the Bible each week? It's not only important that your pastor preaches the Word, but you should be part of a church where its corporate gatherings are filled with reading God's Word, praying God's Word, singing God's Word, and seeing God's Word in the ordinances of baptism and the Lord's Supper.
- Are you continually reminding yourself about what God has done for you in the gospel?

When you dwell in God's Word, he begins to work on your heart, filling you with his Spirit and his Son's love for the hurting. As you help the hurting, remember how precious his grace appeared that hour you first believed. As President Steve once told me and my wife, there is nothing more important than our relationship with God. Grow in your love for the Lord, and you will grow in your love for the hurting. If you're going to help the hurting, you need to walk with God.

· · · · · ·

After taking a couple of chapters to offer encouragement for your soul, the rest of the book turns its attention to how you can practically help those who are hurting.

3

Faithful Friendship

A good friend is hard to come by. No one had a better claim of defending that saying than Job. He was a man who loved God and had great wealth. It is tough to get a grasp of his wealth today, because back in his day wealth consisted of the ownership of animals. Job had a big army of seven thousand sheep and three thousand camels. Living in the Middle East we see camels often. Many times when we're driving cross-country, the traffic is not created by a full highway or a slow car in front of us but by camels loitering in the road. Seeing a camel in the desert is like seeing squirrels in someone's yard in the West. It happens all the time. I've even seen big caravans of several dozen camels in the desert, but I can't get my mind around one man owning three thousand of them. Job also had five hundred yoke of oxen and five hundred female donkeys and plenty of servants to help tend to his animal collection. Job was actually called the greatest of all the people of the East (Job 1:3). That's quite a statement!

Job had it all. It was at this pinnacle of his life that Satan came and disrupted everything. Satan argued that if Job lost his livelihood, he would turn around and curse God. God permitted Satan to go to Job and inflict much pain on him. If anyone truly suffered, it was Job. Four messengers, one after another, came to Job to tell him about the chaos that had come to Job's family and belongings. First, a messenger ran to Job to tell him the oxen were all destroyed by the Sabeans. As soon as that man finished, another messenger ran into Job's house to tell him that a fire had burned up all his sheep and servants. Immediately after that, the news came to Job that a raid came on Job's camels and killed all of them too. And then, if things weren't bad enough, a final man came with the most brutal message. This was the news that no parent ever wants to hear. A great wind came across the wilderness and *all* ten of his children died. Job was living in the middle of the worst nightmare imaginable.

Things didn't get much better for Job in the following days. Not only did he lose his children and his riches, but he also developed sores all over his body. The only relief he found was taking broken pieces of pottery and scraping himself as he sat in a pile of ashes. Talk about being hopeless. His wife was of no help either; her contribution was telling Job to just go ahead and curse God and die.

If anyone was in need of a faithful friend, it was Job. Job must have been hopeful at the arrival of Eliphaz, Bildad, Zophar, and then later Elihu. Job's whole world was crushed. He was the epitome of a hurting man, and his friends had come to see him. Though not the main point of the book, you anticipate witnessing a model of how to love our hurting friends. The bulk of the book traces Job's four friends in their attempt to minister to their hurting friend. However, instead of "Job: A Guide to True Biblical Friendship," we get something closer to "Disaster: How to Hate Your Hurting Friends into Greater Despair." Job's friends accuse, blame, question, and condemn him. Rather than ministering to his suffering, the extended time with his friends was like having salt poured into his open wounds.

The failure of Job's friends brings us to an important question: How can we actually be helpful friends to the hurting people in our lives? What are we to do? There must be a way that we can exhibit love to our friends who are struggling with pain and loss. This chapter will discuss some of the ways you can exhibit faithful friendship for the hurting people in your life who are in need of encouragement.

A Silent Presence

Though Job's friends said some unbiblical and hurtful things to Job (that's a bit of an understatement), they surprisingly did one thing well at the beginning of their time with Job. For the first several days they sympathized with him in an understanding way. Job 2:11–13 tells us of their initial encounters with Job after he suffered the death of his children.

> Now when Job's three friends heard of all this evil that had come upon him, they came each from his own place, Eliphaz the Temanite, Bildad the Shuhite, and Zophar the Naamathite. They made an appointment together to come to show him sympathy and comfort him. And when they saw him from a distance, they did not recognize him. And they raised their voices and wept, and they tore their robes and sprinkled dust on their heads toward heaven. And they sat with him on the ground seven days and seven nights, and no one spoke a word to him, for they saw that his suffering was very great.

Job's friends heard about his suffering and made plans to go to their friend. They generously gave their time, money, and resources to go support Job. When they arrived, they were startled because Job was unrecognizable. The turmoil and suffering had likely changed his appearance dramatically. The text says they showed him sympathy. This clearly involved more than a little hug and a few quick condolences. They didn't come all that way to say, "I'm sorry," and then to depart on their way.

"To show sympathy" means literally "to shake the head."[1] Job wasn't alone in his sorrow; all four men were crying together, shaking their heads in sorrow at the pain Job was feeling. The men were there with Job and hurting alongside him. At the very sight of Job's marred figure, they raised their voices and wept. They tore off their robes and sprinkled dust on their heads. Though not as common as ashes, dust was another sign of mourning.[2] This was an almost over-the-top display of anguish on the part of the friends. Sitting on the ground was another way of showing their sorrow for Job. They sat with their friend and entered into his world of pain and suffering.[3] They were a great example of grieving with someone who was in anguish. All attention was focused not on discussing the problem of evil or analyzing why Job was suffering but on grieving with their friend. These three men sat speechless. For a week! They were a silent presence of encouragement on top of that ash heap of despair.

A man who lost three sons at various times in his life wrote about grief in *The View from a Hearse*:

> I was sitting, torn by grief. Someone came and talked to me of God's dealings, of why it happened, of hope beyond the grave. He talked constantly, he said things I knew were true. I was unmoved, except to wish he'd go away. He finally did. Another came and sat beside me. He didn't talk. He didn't ask leading questions. He just sat beside me for an hour or more, listened when I said something, answered briefly, prayed simply, left. I was moved. I was comforted. I hated to see him go.[4]

There is a kind of ministry that is without words. It is simply being there. Certainly Scripture is the best balm for someone's soul (we'll talk about that later), but there are times when all you need to do for the moment (or for several days) is just sit quietly with someone.

It has often been said that Job's friends were fantastic until they opened their mouths!

But be aware that there is a kind of listening that fails to concentrate on what someone is actually saying. When you and I do this, we presume to know what the other person has to say, and we don't care about what they are really trying to communicate. It's easily noticeable when you are merely looking for a chance to speak. We need to remember that the Bible is not a Band-Aid, and we best not go around slapping our favorite Bible verses on suffering people. Sometimes they just need a friend to be present and understand that this is a difficult time in their life.

We don't take for granted this privilege we have to live among other Christians. Dietrich Bonhoeffer wrote:

> Jesus lived in the midst of his enemies . . . at the end all his disciples deserted him. On the cross he was utterly alone, surrounded by evildoers and mockers. For this cause he had come, to bring peace to the enemies of God. So the Christian, too, belongs not in the seclusion of a cloistered life but in the thick of foes. Not all Christians receive this blessing—the imprisoned, the sick, the proclaimers of the gospel in some lands stand alone, they know that visible fellowship is a blessing. There is so much joy in even a single encounter of brother with brother—how inexhaustible are the riches that open up for those who by God's will are given to us.[5]

I can think of many times when people have been a silent presence for me in my pain. On several occasions, when my pain was at its worst, my friend Ross would just grieve with me. He would simply listen to me groan and complain. If he said anything, he'd just talk about how terrible it was that I was suffering. He called evil "evil." He didn't try to explain it. Listening is a great way to start loving and comforting someone who is suffering. Good friends and counselors understand that oftentimes the best thing they can do is to be quiet and listen. This was the best demonstration of care and sympathy that Job's friends could have shown. They were sympathizers *par excellence* in their week of reverent silence.

True Fellowship

Another way you can help the one who is hurting is to continue opening up about your own life. The one hurting doesn't want to feel like a project or patient but wants to be your genuine friend. Share your heart and what you're learning in your devotional times. Open up with him about your struggles and joys. Continue to include your friend in your life, even if you feel like you are growing more distant because of his painful circumstances. Maintain an atmosphere where honesty is a core component of your relationship.

True fellowship involves both individuals opening up about their lives. One major aspect of this kind of friendship is being honest in our struggle with sin. Fake fellowship allows no one to be a sinner, and so everybody must hide his sin from others. But the fact is, we are all sinners! Jesus's death on the cross attests to this. A distinctly Christian friendship acknowledges that the cross criticizes us more than anyone else can. Looking to the cross liberates us from hiding and instead emphasizes our need for help. We can humbly confess and lay our deepest sinful secrets on the table, laying them bare because Jesus Christ went before us. He suffered the scandalous, public death of a sinner in our place. He was not ashamed to be crucified and laid bare as an evildoer, even though he wasn't one. It is nothing else but our fellowship with Jesus that leads us to the humiliation that comes in confession. As the writer of Proverbs says, "Whoever conceals his transgressions will not prosper, but he who confesses and forsakes will obtain mercy" (28:13). The cross of Christ destroys all pride.

If your sinfulness appears to you in any way smaller or less detestable than the sins of others, you will not open up your life to anyone. You will keep your sins and struggles to yourself, or ignore them entirely. We must instead see our sin as reprehensible in the sight of God. Thomas à Kempis once said, "Never think that thou hast made any progress till thou look upon thyself as inferior to all."[6]

Lay your life bare before your hurting friends. James 5:16 exhorts us to "confess our sins to one another." The mask you wear before men will only leave you and your friend isolated, and it will lead to self-destruction as you hide your sin in the darkness of your heart. Confession is so powerful because in humility it combats and brings a dreadful blow to the pride in your heart. It brings sin into the light. And it will help your hurting friends open up. You are modeling true fellowship for them.

My friend Jeremy was tremendously helpful to me in the days leading up to our church plant. We would meet for accountability and prayer on a regular basis. It was these days when I was particularly struggling in my selfishness and Jeremy modeled true friendship for me. He opened up his life and heart to me, and because of his example I started to do the same. His humility and confession to me and the Lord was a huge encouragement in the dark times. Open up your life and let your friends speak truth into your life. You need their help and they need your help, and it will encourage them when you open up to them in your struggles.

Loyal Friendship

Initially after a loss, injury, or sickness, it seems as though everyone wants to help. But as time goes on, the excitement to help wanes, and the one hurting will often feel neglected and forgotten. There's an important ministry of loyalty, of sticking with the hurting, that can be tremendously helpful, as the writer of Proverbs states:

A man of many companions may come to ruin, but there is a friend who sticks closer than a brother. (18:24)

A friend loves at all times, and a brother is born for adversity. (17:17)

The people you are related to will usually be there for you in adversity. They care, there is family loyalty, there are memories of games at the park. The truth is, however, that you may not get along well; you may not even like each other. The author of these proverbs tells us that a friend is someone who is not only there for you in the difficult times, but he sticks closer to you than a brother because he loves you at all times. These kinds of friends love you in the good, the bad, and the ugly. Friends *decide* to be friends with one another and care for each other in adversity and victory.

It will be tempting for you to leave the side of your friend in his pain and loss. He may no longer be investing in your friendship like he used to. It may be difficult to be with him, and he may even be mean to you. You can quickly begin to feel like you're not getting anything out of the relationship anymore.

This is the story that we often hear when professional athletes go broke after living a life of luxury for years. I read of one basketball player who made over one hundred million dollars during his playing days and always lavished his wealth on his "friends." Everywhere he went, he took an entourage of fifty friends with him to enjoy his money. However, when the money was all gone, so were his friends. He said, "You find out who your real friends are when you see who's left when the money's gone."[7]

I saw this extraordinarily displayed through my wife, Gloria, in our darkest moments. It never ceases to amaze me that she stayed by my side through the most trying times. Her patience and loyalty pointed me to Jesus and allowed me to see my own sin more clearly. She never fought back, but sat by my side in moments of despair.

You have a great ministry opportunity to extend loyalty to your friends when they're in the miry pit and can't seem to get out.

Forgiveness

When you are ministering to those who are hurting, it is inevitable that they will offend you. It may be a spiteful word or a declaration that you are unhelpful or simply a neglect of their normal responsibilities toward you. This was certainly the pattern in my marriage during the most difficult times. I was a difficult man to be around and was constantly berating my wife with comments that were unhelpful and even hurtful. I blamed her for any new pain I experienced and told her that she wasn't doing a good enough job caring for me. She could just have easily reacted in defense or anger back to me and the battle would rage on. These times will come for you, the silent sufferers, and in the midst of them you need to be faithful to the exhortation by Peter: "Do not repay evil for evil or reviling for reviling, but on the contrary, bless, for to this you were called, that you may obtain a blessing" (1 Pet. 3:9).

This is a radical statement. Not only are we not to repay others for their evil, but we are to pay back to people what they don't deserve, namely a blessing. What comes more naturally for us is to want to pay evil back for evil. When you try to inflict pain and justice on another person—whether he deserves it or not—you are saying that God doesn't deserve his throne because you would do a better job. You don't believe God is just, and you place yourself in the position of God as judge. That person may deserve discipline, but we are not the ones who decide or the ones who enact it. Instead, look to the cross and serve the person in spite of his actions. The only way we could be cruel to others is if we forget how compassionate our God has been to us. If Gloria wasn't looking to the cross as strength to forgive me, she wouldn't have made it through our trial.

In the parable of the unforgiving servant, Jesus says we should forgive those who sin against us seventy-seven times. That's Jesus's way of telling us we are to continually forgive those who sin against us. And then he illustrates this with the parable of a king who releases his servant who owed him ten thousand talents. That would have been an astronomical sum in those times. The servant offered to sell himself along with his family and all that he had, but the king let him go and forgave him of the debt. But then that same man went out and found another servant who owed him only one hundred denarii (a relatively tiny sum) and ended up grabbing him and choking him, demanding that he pay him what was owed. The man couldn't pay, and he was put in prison for not paying his debt. Several people witnessed this event and went and told the king about it. The king found the ungrateful servant and put *him* in prison until he paid everything back. Jesus ended the parable by saying, "So also my heavenly Father will do to every one of you, if you do not forgive your brother from your heart" (Matt. 18:35).

In one of our trainings for overseas ministry, a new friend named John said something I'll never forget: "Forgiving flows from forgiven-ness." He said that as we understand more fully that in Christ Jesus we have been forgiven of our sins, we are able to extend true forgiveness to others. Paul states this truth in more than one of his letters:

> God shows his love for us in that while we were still sinners, Christ died for us. (Rom. 5:8)

> Put on then, as God's chosen ones, holy and beloved, compassionate hearts, kindness, humility, meekness, and patience, bearing with one another and, if one has a complaint against another, forgiving each other; as the Lord has forgiven you, so you also must forgive. And above all these put on love, which binds everything together in perfect harmony. (Col. 3:12–14)

The truth is we've all rejected and turned away from the God of the universe by declaring our independence. This disease of the heart called sin doesn't show up on any of our blood tests or X-rays, but it is more paralyzing than any physical disease. We have all told God that we don't need him and have chosen to live our lives according to our own ways. And yet even in our insurrection he sent his one and only Son to die for us. By his gruesome sacrifice on the cross we were set free from our sins and forgiven. John Flavel says:

> Consider how you are daily and hourly wronging God and you will not be so easily inflamed with revenge against those who have wronged you. You are constantly affronting God, yet he does not take vengeance on you, but bears with you and forgives; and will you rise up and avenge yourself upon others?[8]

The mercy of God toward you and me should turn our hearts in mercy for others. How can we now not forgive someone who sins against us?

Forgiving flows from forgiven-ness.

Ministry of Laughter

Every year at our church's anniversary celebration, Glen, one of the pastors on our staff, has a little fun at my expense. Glen is from Australia, and for at least some Australians, the way they show love is through laughter. I may be Australian somewhere back in my family tree because I always feel loved when Glen plays pranks on me at the parties.

Glen's first great prank started when Tom, one of our sound engineers (and current elder), forgot to mute my microphone after I was finished with my sermon at one of our worship gatherings. That would have been bad enough, but he also kept recording my mic feed after my sermon. The combination of these two mistakes, plus the rare event (actually the only time we've ever done this) that we had a solo intro into our next song, led to disaster. After the first verse was sung by Chere (who has a lovely voice), the congregation was to follow in the second verse. The problem was nobody started singing, so being the pastor-leader that I am, I started singing as loudly as I could. The result was epic, and not in a good sense. Chere noted later that it sounded like the speakers were demon-possessed. What ensued was basically a duet with beautifully voiced Chere and tone-deaf Dave. It was awful.

Since Tom recorded the whole thing, Glen decided to play it again for the entire church at our second anniversary celebration. This began the annual tradition of Glen roasting me at these gatherings, and I love it. His roasts have brought joy to my heart in the midst of some difficult times physically and emotionally. I can attest to the truth of Proverbs 17:22 when it says, "A joyful heart is good medicine, but a crushed spirit dries up the bones."

Sometimes a great ministry to people who are hurting is to make them laugh and remind them of the sweet common grace God extends to us. Work hard to find ways to include your friends in something they would enjoy, and lift their spirits. Perhaps the best medicine of all is not found in a prescription from a pharmacy but in a good laugh.

Christ, Our Friend

How are you doing in caring for your hurting friends? Are your relationships similar to that of Job's friends or are you doing better? Are you loving the people God has put in our life? Are you caring for those hurting in a loving way? I'll be the first to confess that at times my heart is cold because I am so consumed with myself, my own agenda, my own schedule, my own rest time, my own to-do list. Me. Me. Me. I must resist this self-centeredness by following Christ's example and obeying his command in John 15:12: "This is my commandment, that you love one another as I have loved you.

Greater love has no one than this, that someone lay down his life for his friends."

Earlier in that same chapter, Jesus tells his disciples that they are no longer servants, but "tonight I call you friends." Tim Keller says that the history of the world can be described in the context of friendship.[9] The Triune God (Father, Son, and Holy Spirit) has existed for eternity in the context of perfect friendship. Then this same God created humans in his image to strive for similar friendship with one another. Even more miraculously, Jesus came to earth to be our friend. He is the ultimate friend who will never leave or forsake us. He is the friend who is faithful at infinite cost to himself so you and I will not be destroyed. Jesus went to the cross where he lost his perfect relationship with the Father so that we can have friendship with the living God. We didn't do anything to deserve it and he doesn't need us to be fulfilled. Our relationship with God is unlike any other. The God of the universe becomes a friend to his enemies.[10]

At the end of his earthly life, Jesus watched his best friends deny and betray him in the garden of Gethsemane. We see ourselves clearly in that story. All have rebelled. We've all betrayed him for the treasures of this world, and yet here is a friend who loves us at all times. A friend who went through the most painful, humiliating, God-rejected death. He faced the ultimate silent treatment—isolated, completely alone, friendless in that moment he died on the cross—so that you could be brought into community with him and called a friend. He is the ultimate friend who, with his nail-pierced arms spread out on the cross, was welcoming you into his life. When you know this, when it sinks deep into your heart, it liberates you to be a friend to those who may reject your love and care. Because Jesus is your friend, you are now able to take rejection from those who may have nothing to give you.[11]

If I know that Jesus has welcomed me into his open arms and

loves me no matter what I do, I can love the hurting even if they hurt me. I can stick by their side even when they have nothing to give me. When Jesus breaks into your life and you've experienced the grace of God, you have hope to befriend the hurting. If you're lonely in your quest to love the hurting, you can be assured that Jesus is the Great High Priest who can sympathize with your life. No one was as lonely as Jesus was there on the cross. On the cross he was abandoned not only by his friends but by God the Father. Jesus became friendless, so that we could be befriended by God. He intends for your friendship with him to be the heartbeat of your friendship with others.

4

Be a Hope Dealer

Several years ago my pain was so bad that my wife reached out to a world-famous doctor in the United States one night over email. To her surprise, he emailed back immediately and let her know that he was opening a clinic in Dubai and that a couple of his protégés would be in Dubai the following week. What are the odds of that? We arranged to meet the doctors in their new clinic here in our city, and they did a comprehensive exam. We asked about the available treatment options they could recommend over here, and they asked back, "Why don't you have surgery with us next week?" This scenario seemed too good to be true, and we saw God's hand "all over it," so-to-speak. Our health insurance miraculously came through at the last possible moment, so I was all set.

We arrived at the hospital with high hopes that this surgery would provide relief for my incredibly painful nerve disorder. I quickly changed into my hospital gown, and I was hooked up to the IV—ready to go. The problem was that no one else was ready for me. Over the course of the day, my surgery kept being postponed hour after hour. Then we were told that we were cutting it close to even have the surgery, because the anesthesiologist on duty was due to head home soon, and the chief surgeon had a flight to catch to leave the country. Apparently the doctors had been delayed due to a difficult surgery that was taking longer than expected, and we anxiously stared at the clock and prayed that my surgery would actually happen.

Finally, eight hours after we arrived at the hospital, I was rolled down to the operating room. I was nervous, but really excited that the surgery was going to happen. I couldn't wait to get some relief at the hands of these amazing physicians who said that I might be shaking hands and playing tennis in no time. I waited outside the operating room for an hour filled with hope because at the time I could hardly use my arms at all.

But then it happened. The doctor emerged from the operating room in his scrubs and told me the devastating news: my surgery was cancelled. There was not enough time or personnel to do the surgery that night, and he was leaving for the airport to head back home. He told me he might be back in a few months. *Maybe.* I was shattered.

As if things couldn't get any worse, the doctors left me alone downstairs for another hour outside the operating room. I was all alone, connected to an IV I didn't need, next to an operating room I would never enter, with no prospect of healing. I was afraid. I felt abandoned. I even let out a loud scream of frustration that apparently no one heard. I had banked my hope on getting relief from the pain and being as good as new. The doctors had said there was an 85 percent chance of total healing, but now with what looked like a 0 percent chance, I was devastated. I had placed my hope in healing, and now that was gone. I had no hope.

Forgetting Jesus

In my hospital bed I had forgotten that my hope is ultimately not in having arms without pain, but in having Jesus. The apostle

Paul understood problems like mine, and—in the book of Galatians—he wrote to the church about his fear that they were departing from the truth of the gospel to have hope in something else. He was baffled that they would do this. Paul wrote to them, "Who has bewitched you? It was before your eyes that Jesus Christ was publicly portrayed as crucified" (3:1). The Galatians were treating the cross as one belief among many in their religion. The cross became incidental and not central. They were putting their works ahead of the most monumental display of love in the history of the world. They were brushing it aside to live according to the law and Paul said it was like they had been bewitched—brainwashed and operating like an insane person who can't think clearly.

Paul reminded them that it was before their very eyes that Christ was portrayed as crucified. Of course the Galatians had not actually seen the crucifixion take place. They lived far from Palestine, and some time had passed since Christ's death. So what does Paul mean? Notice it doesn't say they *saw* Christ crucified but that he *was portrayed* as crucified. This is the idea of something being held up on a sign for everyone to see. Paul is telling them: *Galatians, don't you remember all my preaching to you about Christ? I wasn't just teaching facts or lecturing; I was heralding. I was holding up graphically and vividly the crucifixion. I was bringing the crucifixion from a past event to a present reality.* The Galatians weren't physically present at the crucifixion, but through his preaching Paul brought this past event and its effect into their everyday experience.

Paul showed them the cross. They saw Christ crucified portrayed before their own eyes and made simple for them to understand. It was as if Paul had printed a sign and put the words in capital letters and stuck it up to their faces so they couldn't miss it. It was like a billboard in their town center that said "Christ Alone = Salvation."

Here's what is frightening and sobering. The Galatians knew the truth—they were told the truth, they understood the truth—but then they forgot it. So too, my fundamental problem outside that hospital operating room wasn't that my arms didn't work and they weren't going to get better. It was that I forgot my hope isn't in whether I can play tennis or hold my baby, but in Christ alone. In the midst of my pain I needed someone to remind me of this truth.

Herald the Gospel

As a pastor I have seen the power of God's Word in the lives of others, and as a pastor who struggles with disability, I have felt the power of God's Word in my own time of need. While I'm thankful for modern medicines and the relief they can provide, I understand that my greatest hope doesn't come in a prescription. I know this truth intellectually, but as a person who experiences chronic pain, I need to be reminded of God's sovereign goodness. And those reminders often come through my friends who turn out to be not just friends but hope dealers.

Dietrich Bonhoeffer says that the goal of distinctly Christian friendship is that a friend comes as the "bringer of the message of salvation."[1] He adds,

> Their fellowship is founded solely upon Jesus Christ. Our community with one another consists solely in what Christ has done to both of us. When one person is struck by the word, he speaks it to others. God has willed that we should seek and find his living word in the witness of a brother, in the mouth of man. Therefore, the Christian needs another Christian who speaks God's word to him. He needs him again and again when he becomes uncertain and discouraged, for by himself he cannot help

without belying the truth. He needs his brother to be a bearer and proclaimer of the divine word of salvation.[2]

In my suffering I need the witness of a friend. I need to be encouraged with the fact that God can use me no matter my physical potential. I need to see lightning bolts of God's grace shoot through my depression as I wrestle with nerve pain in the middle of the night. I need to see God's good design in my disability as a means of strengthening me in his grace by reminding me of my need for him. I need those around me to point me to the biblical hope found in the implications of the gospel. I need my friends, my fellow church members, and others to herald the good news to me and to remind me that there is a greater reality at play in my life than just my physical pain.

To minister to your hurting friend effectively, you must know the gospel and its implications well enough to deliberately speak of them to your friend and be able to communicate how the gospel relates to his situation. This ministry is so vital that Paul says in 1 Corinthians 15 that the gospel is of first importance. You have to know it inside and out. First Corinthians 15 is perhaps the best brief summary of the gospel in our Bibles:

> Now I would remind you, brothers, of the gospel I preached to you, which you received, in which you stand, and by which you are being saved, if you hold fast to the word I preached to you—unless you believed in vain.
>
> For I delivered to you as of first importance what I also received: that Christ died for our sins in accordance with the Scriptures, that he was buried, that he was raised on the third day in accordance with the Scriptures, and that he appeared to Cephas, then to the twelve. Then he appeared to more than five hundred brothers at one time, most of whom are still alive, though some have fallen asleep. Then he appeared to James,

then to all the apostles. Last of all, as to one untimely born, he appeared also to me. (1 Cor. 15:1–8)

Just like he reminded the Galatians of the gospel, Paul sets out to remind the Corinthians of the good news he had preached to them. He lays out the content of the gospel—we had sinned against God but Christ died in our place, taking our punishment as the Father poured out his wrath and judgment upon the Son instead of on you and me. He died for our sins and proved that the sacrifice was complete by rising from the dead and appearing to a great multitude. As many have said before me, this was the greatest exchange in all of history.

> But he was wounded for our transgressions;
>> he was crushed for our iniquities;
>> upon him was the chastisement that brought us peace;
>> and with his stripes we are healed.
> All we like sheep have gone astray;
>> we have turned—every one—to his own way;
>> and the LORD has laid on him the iniquity of us all.
>
> (Isa. 53:5–6)

God made him to be sin who knew no sin, so that in him we might become the righteousness of God. (2 Cor. 5:21)

Christ redeemed us from the curse of the law by becoming a curse for us. (Gal. 3:13)

He himself bore our sins in his body on the tree, that we might die to sin and live to righteousness. By his wounds you have been healed. (1 Pet. 2:24)

For Christ also suffered once for sins, the righteous for the unrighteous, that he might bring us to God, being put to death in the flesh but made alive in the spirit. (1 Pet. 3:18)

It is important for us to remind others of these glorious gospel truths. I am well aware of how easily I forget my standing in Christ even as I stare at a thousand Christian books in my office. My job is to teach God's Word, and yet my temptation each day is to forget the gospel. Even if I do remember, my flesh is inclined to resist and rebel. It's easy for me to forget about Jesus. J. Gresham Machen once said:

> What I need first of all is not exhortation, but a gospel, not directions for saving myself but knowledge of how God has saved me. Have you any good news? That is the question that I ask of you. I know your exhortations will not help me. But if anything has been done to save me, will you not tell me the facts?[3]

As my hospital incident unfolded, I quickly forgot the very truth that I was preaching each week to our congregation, and I needed to be reminded of it. I'm not alone in this: there's a legend that Martin Luther was asked why he was preaching on justification by faith for the twentieth time to his congregation. He said he preached on that theme again to the church because they didn't remember it after the nineteenth time. The same is true for me. I need people to encourage me to hold fast to the hope set before us (Heb. 6:18). The gospel is not simply for unbelievers, but it is the very truth that believers—even ones that preach it themselves—need heralded to them each day.

The Gospel for Every Day

Whether your life seems pain-free or pain-full, you should never get over the gospel. Suffering people are inundated with good *advice* all the time. Sometimes they even hear good reports from doctors or others. But somebody needs to bring them good *news*. This is the heart of a Christian's ministry—it's the sharing of good news for the benefit of not only non-Christians but also Christians. Once we follow Christ, we don't move on from the gospel to more advanced stuff. There is no spiritual quantum physics to move to beyond the gospel. As redeemed sinners, we never get beyond this. It is our job to bring everything in our lives "in line" with the thrust and direction of the gospel. Our work is a continual realignment process.[4]

We need to point our friends to God's instances of tenderness and care over them in the past. A Bible professor once told me that God's faithfulness in the past is both a model and a promise of his faithfulness in the future, but that God is way too creative to do things the same way twice.[5] If God has saved us through the death and resurrection of Christ, how will he not provide deliverance in the future (Rom. 8:31–39)? When you think about it that way, it seems preposterous to suggest that God would abandon his children.

Because of the finished work of Christ, you can remind your exhausted and discouraged wife that Jesus understands what she is going through. He carried the heaviest burden that could ever be— the sin of all those who would place their faith in him—and he bore that burden so that she would never have to carry it even an inch.

When our aging parents face death, we can remind them that because Christ conquered death and rose from the grave three days later, death will not be the final story of their lives. There is soon coming a day for them when they will be face to face with their Savior. Death is a defeated enemy who can only serve God's good purposes, decrepit as dying is. Remind the aging that the happiness of heaven commences immediately after death.[6] Through the death and resurrection of Christ, they have been reconciled to God and will live forever in that heavenly city.

When a church member is facing her greatest fear and learns that she has stage four cancer, you can tell her that God is worth trusting still. Remind her that Jesus trusted God the Father when he faced the greatest fear anyone could ever face. In the garden of

Gethsemane he suffered anguish at the holy wrath that was coming. Jesus went to the cross and faced utter and total rejection from God. It was a complete severing from the Father. It was the greatest fear anyone could face, and he faced that fear for God's glory and our salvation. Jesus faced the ultimate fear so that we can face our fears by faith.

You can tell a friend who is depressed that he will see his darkness lifted and will one day sing of his never-ending gladness. That because of Christ's agonizing dark night in Gethsemane and his faithfulness to go to the cross, his dark nights of the soul will be but a memory. The anxieties of the morning will be long gone. Christ's nail-scarred hands will wipe our tear-stained eyes dry forever.

For the neighbors who are being persecuted for their faith because they were born with a certain passport and live amidst violence, remind them that Jesus faced the greatest persecution in order to give us his birthright. Through our faith in him we have a new citizenship, a birthright, and an inheritance that is ours forever and not subject to immigration proceedings or legal red tape. There is coming a day when as citizens of this new heavens and new earth, we will have perfect peace, and persecution will be impossible because we will all love God.

There is coming a day when we will be with Jesus. This is what we have to look forward to. To be with the Savior who was pierced for us. To be with our Lord who gave his life so we could have life— the one who suffered so we could be united with God. We will be with him. This is future grace. We all need the gospel, but times of hurt can be the most important times when we need to be reminded that our hope exists outside of ourselves. Our hope is grounded in the past, secure in the future, and available for us today. Don't let your friends splash around in the puddles of fake hope that make up the world's humanistic religions. Encourage them to believe the distinctively Christian promise of future grace—where a tidal wave of Christ's love is poured out on us for eternity.[7]

No Need for Eloquence

You may not be the most eloquent speaker and you may not be ordained in ministry, but if you are a believer, you are gifted with the Holy Spirit and the gospel. All our other circumstances and feelings may change, but God and his gospel always remain the same. Remember the truth of Romans 1:16: "For I am not ashamed of the gospel, for it is the power of God for salvation to everyone who believes, to the Jew first and also to the Greek."

The gospel is powerful regardless of who speaks it or how eloquent they are in sharing it. In fact, the Bible only attributes the phrase "the power of God" in reference to Jesus Christ himself and the gospel. That's it. Pastor Milton Vincent writes, "Outside of heaven, the power of God in its highest density is found inside the Gospel. . . . Such a description indicates that the gospel is not only powerful, but that it is the ultimate entity in which God's power resides and does its greatest work."[8]

The thing I needed most walking out of the hospital that night after my failed attempt at surgery was to be reminded of this powerful truth. I needed a hug, but I also needed my mind and heart realigned with the truth of God. There are times in helping others when you need be quiet and listen. Remember Job's friends? They should have remained quiet longer. But—in this moment of mine—I needed to be reminded that my hope was not in my health but in Jesus. Gloria shared with me these thoughts in the hospital room, and then on the way to the car a fellow pastor reminded me that Christ is sufficient and that God is both compassionate and in control over my life. I needed that powerful perspective, even if it was hard for me to hear in the moment. I needed to be reminded of the permanency of the gospel in my life: health conditions change, but Jesus and my redemption in him are unchanging.

I once read a story about how Charles Spurgeon's grandfather preached for him one night. Spurgeon, the great British preacher, was running late getting to the church. By the time he got there, his grandfather had already started preaching. Young Spurgeon was already widely known at that time, and when he walked in, his grandfather paused his sermon and said something to the effect of: "Okay, everyone, take a look. My grandson is here now, the great Charles Haddon Spurgeon; he may be a greater preacher than I, but he can't preach a greater gospel."[9] This point remains true today. All Christians are stewards of the same gospel message. We have been given no better message and no greater news. Jesus rose from the dead. Jesus is alive today, and we are certain that Jesus will return. Proclaiming the gospel is not just the job of professionals, but any believer in simple language can speak this truth with love and compassion to a hurting friend.

A Word about Your Nonbelieving Friends

I realize that you may be seeking to care for friends and relatives who are not Christians. We all have hurting people in our lives who have not repented of their sin and trusted in Christ for salvation. While this book is primarily written to Christians who are ministering to other Christians, this same message of hope should be held out to nonbelievers. What if the Lord would use your friend's trial to draw him or her to repentance and faith in Christ? A quick reading of the Bible will inevitably lead to an encounter with so-called unlikely converts who were miraculously saved by God. The apostle Paul remembers his conversion: "But when he who had set me apart before I was born, and who called me by his grace, was pleased to reveal his Son to me . . . " (Gal. 1:15–16).

Paul hated God. He was like a terrorist—arresting, persecuting, and killing Christians for their faith. Yet there he was on the road to Damascus, on his way to persecute more Christians, when God came to him. In God's intimate love and care for Paul, it pleased him to reveal his Son, and Paul saw Jesus as the true Son of God. Paul's conversion wasn't the result of any kind of educational process. He was going down the road to Damascus and got slammed down to the ground in his tracks. He was blinded, and God transformed him in a moment.

Be encouraged that God can save anyone at any time. If you have hurting people in your life whom you think it would take a miracle to save because they're so hard-hearted, then you're right. It would be a miracle, just as the Bible attributes the conversion of any one of us. Each of our conversions testifies to the fact that it is God who saves miraculously. Persistently pray that God would let light shine in their hearts as you graciously speak to them about the hope they can have in Christ.

And as you encourage them with the gospel and pray for their hearts, remember that Christ gave us an example of service that applies to believers and unbelievers alike. That's what the next chapter is all about.

5

Serve Like Jesus

The disciples were gathered around the table to eat the Passover meal, but there was a problem. Nobody had washed their feet. Now that may sound funny to us today. Probably no one in your house scrubs your feet with a sponge before you eat dinner. But foot washing was a necessary custom in those days. The roads weren't paved, and humans had to share the roads with animals. You can probably imagine the gross things that covered the roads. Sandals could hardly protect against the dirt and bacteria, and by the end of the day your feet would end up being quite repulsive. And since there were no private showers or baths, you'd go to the village bathhouse to get cleaned up before you went to dinner. Each of the disciples had already been to the bathhouse that night in preparation for the meal. The problem was that they still had to walk from the bathhouse to the banqueting room, and now their feet were dirty again. How is this problem normally solved? In most homes the job of foot washing was reserved for a lowly servant who was stationed at the door with a bucket of water and a towel. But the disciples were borrowing a room so there wasn't a host or servant to wash their feet.[1] Why didn't one of the disciples jump in and do it? They probably felt like the job was below their pay grade. To be honest, the last thing a guy wants to do is to wash another guy's feet. It's not the type of ministry that would rally an overwhelming surge of volunteers. The disciples were aware that someone needed to wash the others' feet. They just didn't want to do it for each other, and apparently they didn't even want to wash their *own* feet.

The disciples' minds were far from the place of servanthood. They weren't busy dreaming up ways to serve one another. Instead of volunteering to serve and wash feet, they had the audacity to argue with one another about which of them was the greatest. It seems obvious that if there's a disagreement at dinner with Jesus present, and you're wondering who has the greatest résumé of the group, you'd give Jesus the award. However, they were arguing about their own greatness in front of the one who left his place of glory in heaven to be with them. It's hard to imagine a greater contradiction.

It was in that context this Jesus redefined humble service. "[Jesus] rose from supper. He laid aside his outer garments, and taking a towel, tied it around his waist. Then he poured water into a basin and began to wash the disciples' feet and to wipe them with the towel that was wrapped around him" (John 13:4–5). By laying aside his outer garment, Jesus was taking the role of a servant. And like a servant, Jesus got down low to the ground to reach their feet.

Awkwardness and embarrassment surely would have filled the room as he slowly washed their feet . . . one by one. It was such a lowly act that it was actually illegal to have a Jewish servant do it, and so it was absolutely shocking that Jesus did it. He laid aside his glory and took on the form of a servant to clean the feet of men he created.[2] This is the God who says in Isaiah that he can turn rivers into islands. He's the one who can turn darkness into light. He is the one who merely spoke and things came into existence. And this same God kneels down to wash John's feet. And James's feet. And

Andrew's feet. And even Judas's feet, his enemy who was ready to turn him over to the authorities that very night.

The act of foot washing pointed to the greatest act of humility and service in the history of the world. There in the upper room we have a glimpse of what Jesus did on the cross. The disciples were expecting a military messiah, and instead they had a suffering servant who would humbly lay down his life in weakness and shame to cleanse his people's sin. But the incredibly shocking incident didn't stop there. After the incident Jesus said, "Do you understand what I have done to you? You call me Teacher and Lord, and you are right, for so I am. If I then, your Lord and Teacher, have washed your feet, you also ought to wash one another's feet. For I have given you an example, that you also should do just as I have done to you" (John 13:12–15).

Jesus washing the disciples' feet is a picture of his ultimate service on the cross, but it is also a model for how we serve as Christians. Jesus is telling us that our service should be characterized by the humility found in foot washing. As we help those who are hurting, we need to take time to reflect on how astounding this act of service really was and recalibrate our hearts to be ready to serve our friends like Jesus served. In this chapter we'll look at specific ways we can serve our hurting friends.

Serve in Lowly Ways

Jesus was ready to do the lowliest of acts for the lowliest of people in the most inconvenient of times. He was about to die and face the wrath of God for our sins, yet he spent the night washing the feet of his enemy. This should be your paradigm as you seek to serve those who are hurting. Some service is rather easy to do. It's easy to do things for others when we expect to receive something from them. But there is nothing distinctly Christian about serving in order to get acclaim, acknowledgment, or recognition. When our aim in service is to bring earthly glory to ourselves, Jesus says we have our reward in full (Matt. 6:2). Distinctly Christian love and service is a humble, selfless love that says I want your best even if it costs me. When we serve those who are depressed, disabled, handicapped, and hurting, we're going to have to serve without need for recognition or thanksgiving. Our giving of service cannot be dependent on the response we get. Distinctly Christian service must be humble and lowly, and we must aim to honor the Lord if we want to look like Jesus.

It's stunning that Jesus would wash Judas's feet even though that same man would betray him later that very night. He didn't wash Peter's feet and then skip over Judas to get to James. This has many implications for our lives:

- This means we serve the hurting people in our families regardless of division or hurt feelings.
- We serve hurting people cross-culturally. Indians show sacrificial love to Pakistanis. Latin Americans to African Americans. Caucasians to Asians, and so on. No image bearer of any ethnicity is above serving another image bearer of another ethnicity. All of us are made in the image of God and have dignity.
- We serve across gender lines. Men serve women. Women serve men. There's not one gender that's off the hook from serving the hurting.
- We serve cross-occupational lines. Doctors serve construction workers. Hospitality staff serve lawyers. Engineers serve tennis instructors. We make no distinction based on employment.
- We serve cross-economic lines. The rich serve the poor and the poor serve the rich.
- We serve cross-family-status lines. Grandparents are not greater than parents who are not greater than young

married couples who are not greater than singles who are not greater than youth. We serve people in all stages of life.

There is no pecking order in the body of Christ. There is no section for the VIPs—no one is exempt from a certain area of service because of earthly status. According to God, we are equal coheirs in the body of Christ under Jesus, our head. We all serve everybody, including and especially those who are hurting and have nothing to give us. Serving God with this kind of humility shows the world that our God is worthy to be served. We are willing to go so low and wash feet because he is so great.

Imagine a picture of what this would look like for the hurting if Christians lived this out all over the world. Massive numbers of orphans are being adopted. The disabled are being assisted. Young moms with postpartum depression are being supported, loved, and cared for. We never wonder whether the elderly and widowed are provided for because the body of Christ is all over it. Pastors of churches are willing to clean the bathroom of an elderly man who lives alone. A son joyfully changes out the bedpan and bathes his father, who is dying of cancer. If we're going to follow the example of Jesus's service in caring for the hurting, then we must volunteer for the lowliest of jobs. One thing that will help us in doing lowly service is thinking accurately about ourselves. Thomas à Kempis said, "This is the highest and most profitable lesson, truly to know and to despise ourselves. To have no opinion of ourselves and to think always well and highly of others."[3] The apostle Paul understood this: "For by the grace given to me I say to everyone among you not to think of himself more highly than he ought to think, but to think with sober judgment, each according to the measure of faith that God has assigned" (Rom. 12:3).

We must understand our sinfulness in order to serve the lowliest of positions. If my sinfulness appears to me in any way smaller or less detestable in comparison with the sins of others, I'm still not recognizing my sinfulness at all. Only when we see our sin as the worst and God's grace through the cross as amazing, will we sink down into the depths of humility in serving others. Only then will we allow ourselves and our agenda to be disturbed by the needs of the people around us.

Serve with Your Words

I vividly remember the day I preached my first sermon. I was nervous that morning in New England, and even today when I think about it I can feel my heart beating a bit faster. It was an interesting sermon to say the least. I put a big cardboard box on the platform and surrounded it with yellow caution tape. I walked up to the pulpit and said, "What I have in the box is the most dangerous thing in the world." I reached inside and pulled out a long knife. I said that the knife can be a dangerous weapon. It has been used to shed blood over the course of centuries. But even though it can be a powerful weapon, the knife is not the most dangerous thing in the world. I walked back to the box and pulled out a loaded gun and pointed it at those sitting in the front row. Of course, it was loaded with water and it glowed in the dark, but nonetheless I got the point across as I squirted water on a couple of the youth sitting in the front row. I said that guns can be lethal, but there is something even more dangerous than a gun. I walked back to the box one last time. This time I put on a pair of yellow gloves and stuck my hands in the box and picked up a slimy, gray object and held it out to the congregation. As a few members in the front row gasped and closed their eyes, I said, "Friends, this is the most dangerous thing in the world."[4]

And then I read this verse: "The tongue is a fire, a world of unrighteousness . . . it is a restless evil, full of deadly poison" (James 3:6, 8).

I held out to the congregation a large, fresh buffalo tongue. This disgustingly effective sermon illustration was the result of my wife's diligent efforts to track down a cow's tongue from the local butchers. No cow tongues were available, but the local buffalo butcher was happy to sell us a buffalo tongue. The point I was making was obvious. The tongue is a dangerous thing. Words can kill. Proverbs 12:18 says, "There is one whose rash words are like sword thrusts."

Words have the power to wound. They have the power to damage the hearer. When you stab someone with a sword, you can take the sword out, but you can't take out the wound. Reckless words lead to wounds and scars. Once a word is uttered . . . it's uttered; it can never be as if it wasn't said. You can't swallow it or take it back. There is no rewind function on our words or a magic erase button. This much is obvious now that we live in the digital communication age, where our digital trail of clicks and words are recorded and time-stamped. And if we're honest with ourselves, we can't stop a conversation and say, "I'm so sorry I said that. I didn't mean it." You can't say that because it wouldn't be true—you said it and therefore you meant to say it. There wasn't a little alien living inside you forcing you to say it. The more honest response would be to say that you're sorry for saying exactly what you feel *but you just wish you hadn't said it out loud.*

Words are like poisonous venom, like toxic chemicals that bring pollution to the air. But there is hope. Look at the rest of Proverbs 12:18: "but the tongue of the wise brings healing."

It's interesting that while the stabbing of a sword comes in an instant and is devastating, wise words can bring healing. And yet healing is not something that comes instantly. When you have surgery, you are cut, but then there are antibiotics and pain medication to take and exercises you must do. It takes time and effort to recover. It is the same with healing words—it's an ongoing regimen of wise words that can bring healing to one's soul. Healing words need to become the ongoing quality of our speech. A steady diet of life-giving words can bring healing to your hurting friend. Look at these verses that show how our words bring life:

> That the mouth of the righteous is a fountain of life. (Prov. 10:11)

> Let no corrupting talk come out of your mouths, but only such as is good for building up, as fits the occasion, that it may give grace to those who hear. (Eph. 4:29)

Many of our church members have done an outstanding job of encouraging me with their words. Sue is always ready to lend an encouraging word. Here is one of many emails she has sent to encourage me in the midst of my trial.

> Hi Dave,
>
> What a great day!! We really enjoyed Josh's teaching and have certainly gone away with some big thoughts and challenges! And the picnic was fun. I had a chance to chat with Gloria, so that was great. She is such a treasure!
>
> This morning I was thinking about Habakkuk 3:16–19 and was thinking about you and your pain. Habakkuk writes, "I hear, and my body trembles; my lips quiver at the sound; rottenness enters into my bones; my legs tremble beneath me. Yet I will quietly wait for the day of trouble to come upon people who invade us. Though the fig tree should not blossom, nor fruit be on the vines, the produce of the olive fail and the fields yield no food, the flock be cut off from the fold and there be no herd in the stalls, yet I will rejoice in the Lord; I will take joy in the God of my salvation. God, the Lord, is my strength; he makes my feet like the deer's; he makes me tread on my high places."
>
> Habakkuk is such a good example. There were so many bad things happening, but he chose to trust in the Lord! He allowed God to be his strength and take him to the high places. I like

that! Have a great week and keep enjoying your visitors in the busyness!

God's blessings, Sue

I love how she pointed me to Scripture and gave me encouragement from God's Word. This is her normal pattern. Julie also emails me often, letting me know that she is praying for me and others in the congregation and asking for prayer requests for those suffering. Bessie and Sarah let me know they're praying for me. My friend Colin in Australia actually handwrote a three-page letter from Sydney and posted it via the snail mail all the way to Dubai. It was incredibly encouraging!

How are you doing with your words? Are you building up others with wise words of healing? Are you deliberate about how you speak to the hurting? Do you apologize when your words are reckless? Do you write letters of encouragement to those facing challenging situations? Are you letting your distraught friends know that you are thinking about them by giving them a phone call? It's amazing how a well-timed word of encouragement can be the beginning of healing for your friends.

Serve in Unique and Specific Ways

Another way to serve your hurting friends in a Christlike way is to figure out unique ways to minister to their specific situations. Our good friends, David and Kris, are unbelievable at finding ways they can uniquely help someone who is hurting. With my handicap, I can't drive or lift up my kids so it makes life very difficult, especially when Gloria is sick or when she has car trouble. On a number of occasions, David and Kris have kept our children at their house for a sleepover and then taken them to school and later dropped them off at home. On a couple of occasions they've kept our daughters for several days while my wife was traveling. Another friend and fellow staff member, Corsaire, has gone out of her way early in the morning to pick up our kids twice a week to get them to school. This is an incredible relief for my wife, who isn't particularly fond of driving the two-and-a-half hours it takes to do drop-off and pick-up every day. Another friend, Angela, volunteered to keep our eighteen-month-old son for four days while Gloria traveled to the United States. I wasn't able to watch our toddler (toddlers require a lot of lifting, scrubbing, catching, and other arm-intensive work), and it was obvious that if Gloria was going to be able to serve in this rare ministry opportunity, I would need some special help. It was certainly not a convenient time for Angela—her husband was also traveling, she has two children of her own, and she was in her first trimester of pregnancy. But she served joyfully and selflessly!

My wife, Gloria, has also done an amazing job serving me in the midst of my depression and disability. For those early years of my depression, she worked hard to bring joy to my heart. She knows that one of my favorite things is surprises. I love surprising people, and I love being surprised. Believe it or not, God has used this in my darkest times to minister to me! Gloria's best surprises involved letting me know that she was pregnant. If you are a parent, you probably remember exactly where you were when you discovered you would be blessed by a new addition in the next nine or so months. One time my wife handed me a pregnancy test at the top of the steps to the art museum in Philadelphia where Rocky did the famous run up the steps. One year on Father's Day, my two kids handed me a card with a sonogram picture while we were enjoying the view at the top of the Burj Khalifa (the world's tallest building). I felt so loved that my wife kept another secret (strange statement, isn't it?) for over a week when she was due with our fourth. She wrote the good news into one of her books. She handed me a rough draft for *Treasuring Christ When Your Hands Are Full* and asked me to read it, knowing that I would eventually get to the surprise. Apparently I'm a slow reader, but finally I burst into happy tears while reading the book. These joyful surprises were a great gift to me in hard times.

Sacrificial service is marked by a selflessness that takes the time to truly know the person's needs. When you're caring for a hurting individual, one way you can demonstrate your love is by knowing people well and looking for unique opportunities to serve them. I'm thankful Gloria and others have worked hard to understand ways to show how much they care about me.

Four Questions to Diagnose Your Heart

If you're struggling in your service to a hurting friend or family member, it might be helpful to ask yourself the following questions:

1. Do I Get Upset If No One Recognizes Me for My Service?

If this upsets you, then it's quite possible you're not serving for God's glory but for your own. If you're serving and at the same time you're looking over your shoulder hoping someone will notice you, then you're doing it for the wrong reasons. Jesus has promised to be with you to the end of the age (Matt. 28:20), and surely he is with you in your selfless service to others for his glory. You will not be disappointed when Christ is revealed in all his glory! Boldly walk by faith in his promises, and serve with the strength he supplies so he alone gets the glory. God is most glorified in your service when people see the Savior through the servant. If you're serving so that the hurting person showers you with gratitude or gifts, then you're not serving in a Christlike way.

How do you know you're working for other people's recognition? You feel like quitting if you're underappreciated or overwhelmed with the task. You are distraught when no one acknowledges your humility. If your motive is to please God and accomplish his will, then what your hurting friends say or don't say won't make a big difference to you. If your motive for serving is anything other than the glory of God, it is not distinctly Christian service. Look to Christ, who suffered in your place, and by faith see him exalted to the right hand of the Father. This Christ has both the authority and the willingness to give you everything you need to serve him for his glory. The day is coming when everyone will recognize Jesus for who he is, so serve him today with joy!

2. Am I Ever Inconvenienced in My Service?

We've often decided the ways we'll serve based on our own terms. I'm willing to serve someone in need when it's convenient for me, in areas that I enjoy, or in ways that won't eat away at other things I'd rather do. We may say in our hearts, "Lord, I'll serve any need in any place except _____." You may be willing to give someone a ride when you're already heading that direction, but if it means changing your schedule, you remain silent. Or you may be ready to make someone a meal because you love cooking and at the same time not really take care of the person's actual needs. You do only what's easy for you. But as a Christian, you are called to inconvenience yourself for the sake of others. This is what it means to "bear one another's burdens." If you're truly doing it, then some or all of the weight of that person's burden actually comes upon you. Distinctly Christian service occurs when you aren't concerned with your needs or preferences, but with what will help build up the person you aim to serve. Trust that your Father in heaven is a good Father, and he is ever gracious to you, even in the times when he brings difficult service opportunities into your life. Walking by faith, put one foot in front of the other in the path of joyful obedience to love your neighbor.

3. Do I Feel Too Embarrassed to Be Treated Like a Servant?

Maybe you think you're too good for a task. For most of us the worst thing isn't necessarily doing a menial task; it's being treated like a servant. I'll do the lowest task if I'm treated like I'm great. But the minute I'm treated like a servant, that's it. John 13:16 says, "Truly, truly, I say to you, a servant is not greater than his master, nor is a messenger greater than the one who sent him."

Jesus was telling his disciples in the upper room that as his students, they were certainly not greater than their teacher, so they could look forward to being like him. The works God had for them to carry out toward one another would be similar to what Jesus himself had done. Their works would involve humble service even to the point of being treated like a servant.

Maybe the role you've been given toward your hurting friend is embarrassing and even demeaning. You think it should be left to "those" people to do. Friend, the humble servant feels no jealousy. He or she can praise God when others are preferred, because they've learned that they are nothing without Christ. In your lowly service to others, rejoice that you are in very good company. To be meek and humble like our Lord is a sweet thing. Believe this by faith, and take up the foot-washing basin with your dear Savior.

4. Do I Complain about the Ministry of Serving Others That God Has Given Me?

Are you going about your work begrudgingly? Are you constantly letting the hurting know how hard you're working and how it's interrupting the life you prefer to live? Are you drawing attention to your service by making it known how hard it is to do what you do? All of these things are just drawing out the selfishness that is deep down in your heart.[5] All of us need regular perspective adjustments—even by the hour! Remind yourself of your Savior's selfless sacrifice on your behalf, and realize that Christ is the One who empowers your service to others by his Spirit. What do you have that you have not been given by God? What a cheerful thing it is to be given gifts to give to others for the sake of serving Jesus.

The Power for Selfless Service

Maybe you've asked yourself those questions and you realize that you're struggling at serving in a way that honors Christ. How do we get the strength to do this? On our own, selfless Christlike service is impossible and unattainable. We can only love in these ways because God first loved us. We can humble ourselves because God humbled himself. Jesus came not to be served but to serve, and while we were sinners he gave his life as a ransom for many (Mark 10:45).

We can go low in our service because in Christ we are eternally rich. We can be nothing, because we know that apart from Christ we are nothing. But through the life and death of Christ we've been given everything we have as a gift. Your significance, security, and eternal glory are yours without risk of losing it. This same gospel that encourages the hurting needs to be rehearsed in your own mind and heart. Remembering this truth fuels your service especially in the difficult situations you find yourself in. Only then can you turn and do the most menial tasks without caring what others think about you. Only then can you share healing words of encouragement again and again because the gospel is always true. Only then can you find the energy to serve in unique ways out of true love for the hurting that comes not from their acceptance of you but from your acceptance in Christ. Only then can you serve like Jesus.

6

The Power of God in Prayer

I am a conference junkie. Gathering together with hundreds and sometimes thousands of other believers for several days of worship, teaching, and fellowship is my idea of a really great time. However, when one conference from a couple of years ago comes to mind, it isn't the amazing speakers or music that I most remember, but a brief conversation I had in the lobby on my way out to dinner one evening. I was standing by the front doors when a couple of pastors and their wives approached me. One of the wives, Becky, acknowledged that she was hoping to meet me at the conference. In fact, she and her husband had prayed together that morning that they would run into me. Becky told me that she had read Gloria's latest book and heard about the pain and suffering I had dealt with in my arms. She began to tell me about her own struggles with terrible arm pain. Her disorder was similar to mine, and she had gotten to the place where she could hardly move her helpless arms and had a device implanted in her back to help manage the pain.

Becky recalled how one day someone decided to pray over her for healing. The one who was praying asked God to make it clear that he was healing her. During the prayer Becky's device in her back shut off completely. It had never done that before, and there was no logical reason why it did that and no way it could shut off on its own. After the device turned off, Becky felt absolutely no pain. The pain has been 100 percent gone since that time, and she's had full use of both of her arms without any other treatments. She hasn't had the device taken out and is keeping it as a "stone of remembrance" of what God has done in healing her.

Becky's point in telling me her story was to urge me to not give up praying. She wanted me to know that my prayers were not a useless or meaningless duty, but that God in his kindness ordained that he would act when we pray. I walked back to my hotel room that night realizing that I had actually stopped praying for healing. As the years passed by, I gave up praying for healing and just settled into the new reality of my painful existence. Becky's story was just the jolt that I needed to remind me that God is all-powerful and could heal me. And that the God of the universe actually listens to our prayers. Scottish pastor Robert Murray M'Cheyne once said, "If I could hear Christ praying for me in the next room, I would not fear a million enemies. Yet distance makes no difference. He is praying for me."[1] Jesus Christ the King of the world has all authority over disease and is right now interceding for us before the Father. The thought of this should light our hearts on fire with hope. Those struggling in pain need to be reminded that there are no renegade molecules in the world, no DNA strand, no nerve disorder that isn't under his authority. God can miraculously heal, and most often when he does, it corresponds with the prayers of his people.

The Sun Stood Still

The power of prayer is remarkably illustrated in chapter 10 of the book of Joshua. Israel had signed a peace treaty with a Canaanite city named Gibeon. The defection of this important city causes anxiety among several other Canaanite leaders and a partnership is formed, led by Adoni-zedek. Joshua now controlled four key cities, and so Adoni-zedek builds this coalition, and they go to fight for control over this strategic area that provided access to the coast.

Things go awry very quickly for this army in their battle against Israel. God throws this coalition into a great panic, the Israelites attack, and there is a colossal slaughter. As the coalition retreats from Israel, even more are killed in a massive hailstorm. Imagine the scene as Joshua looked over the battlefield. On the one hand the panicking enemy was running away and on the other hand the sun was descending. Joshua had the opportunity to end the battle right then but time was not on his side. What was Joshua going to do? Would he resign and give up on finishing off his enemies that day knowing that they could escape in the darkness?

Rather than calling it a day and stop the battle, Joshua did something incredible: he prayed and asked God to prolong the day. He asked God to stop the solar clock from ticking. Joshua had a prayer request that would rock any modern-day prayer meeting.

On the day the Lord gave the Amorites over to Israel, Joshua said to the Lord in the presence of Israel:

"Sun, stand still at Gibeon,
   And moon, in the valley of Aijalon."
And the sun stood still, and the moon stopped,
   until the nation took vengeance on their enemies.
   (Josh. 10:12–13)

Now, it doesn't take a genius to see that this was an unbelievable prayer. Joshua had the courage to ask God to stop time on behalf of his people, and God answered by suspending the sun and the moon in that very moment. The coalition's hopes to hide in the darkness never came, and they were defeated.

While our requests may not be this dramatic, I hope it never ceases to amaze us that God listens to the voice of the man or woman who comes to him. It's unfathomable. We should never stop marveling that the one who is seated on high stoops down and bends his ear to dust and ashes. God decisively intervenes for his people. In this instance he threw hailstones down at the enemy. He stopped the sun so they could finally defeat them. God did what was impossible for the Israelites and provided them victory that day. The question screams out at us as we read that passage: why don't we ask God for the impossible? For the spread of the gospel, church planting, healing from the pain of the loss of a loved one, the reconciliation of a marriage, freedom from depression, or healing from a disease?

God Moves through Prayer

Depending on our backgrounds, some of us need to be reminded that God actually moves through prayer. There is at times a reaction against those who say that our prayers can actually change God's mind. It is true, we can't change God's mind. And God doesn't change his pre-ordained plans because we pray. The Scripture is clear about this:

> God is not man, that he should lie, or a son of man, that he should change his mind. Has he said, and will he not do it? Or has he spoken, and will he not fulfill it? (Num. 23:19)

> Jesus Christ is the same yesterday and today and forever. (Heb. 13:8)

> Every good gift and every perfect gift is from above, coming down from the Father of lights with whom there is no variation or shadow due to change. (James 1:17)

And then just to make it unmistakably clear, God says in Malachi 3:6, "For I the LORD do not change." This is the theological doctrine of the immutability of God. God is never changing. So the purpose of prayer is not to change God's plan.

Maybe you've also heard that God changes our hearts in prayer, and so that's why we pray. It is sometimes said that prayer doesn't actually do anything outside of ourselves, but we pray because it changes us. Well, that's only partially true. Prayer does change us. God uses our times of prayer to reveal sin in our lives and to awaken our hearts to his will. But that's not the only reason we pray, and it doesn't get to the heart of prayer.

Why do we pray to a God who is sovereign over the universe? We pray because prayer is God's sovereignly chosen instrument in which he moves in our lives. Before the foundation of the world, God chose that he would use the prayers of his people to be the engine of his work in the world.

I'm always helped by understanding that the reason we pray is similar to the reason we share the gospel with nonbelievers. One might say, "Well, if God has elected and chosen whom he'll save, and this saving will definitely come to pass, then we don't need to share our faith. It won't really affect anything." But you see—God in his sovereign plan has determined that the primary way the chosen ones will come to faith is through the sharing of the gospel by his people. And so God elects, God plans, God reigns sovereignly over everything, *but* we share the gospel and people come to faith. Though God brings his people to salvation, we're the means by which he does it. And so we go out and share our faith with everyone, boldly. As we share we don't know who will come to faith, but we know that some will come to faith. It is with the same faithfulness that we pray. While all that comes to pass has been ordained by God, he has also sovereignly ordained that the prayers of his people would be the way in which he works in the world. His sovereignty doesn't negate our responsibility to act in prayer. Friend, your prayers are not in vain. Don't stop praying. God may not always answer our prayers in the way we would like, but prayer is God's way of moving in and through us.

Praying for Your Friends

Praying for our hurting friends is certainly one of the very best ways we can help them. Dietrich Bonhoeffer says, "True spiritual love will speak to Christ about a brother even more than to a brother about Christ. It knows that the most direct way to others is always through prayer to Christ and that love of others is wholly dependent upon the truth in Christ."[2] We often tell people (especially when we don't know what else to say), "Oh . . . I'm so sorry. I'll be praying for you." We say it to communicate our care and concern for them, but how fervent and faithful are we in actually praying for them? If you're anything like me, then you probably forget your promise to pray for many of these situations.

When you promise to pray for someone, it's usually best to go ahead and pray right then and there. As you finish a conversation or even a phone call, tell the person you'd like to pray at that moment. It is incredibly encouraging to the wounded soul to hear a brother or sister in Christ pray for them.

And when you pray for people during a personal devotional time, go ahead and tell them. Share with them what Scripture passage you used to pray for them or the contents of your prayers. Perhaps send them a note letting them know you were thinking of them and praying for them. I was grateful to receive this email from Aaron, a fellow church member:

> Pastor Dave,
>
> I would like to take this opportunity to thank you for the time and effort you are putting in serving our Great I Am through serving us. You are a living testimony of God's grace along with all the pastors and elders and staff of Redeemer

Dubai. You are all a huge blessing for someone like me. I am so thankful to God for bringing me to my home here in Dubai—Redeemer Church of Dubai. My best blessing this year is when God brought me to the church to be united with my brothers and sisters in Christ.

I am always looking forward to our worship gathering and always being amazed that I am singing along with the congregation and sitting there listening to the Gospel. It is so amazing, and it is unbelievable that someone like me would be called by God into His fellowship and into the fellowship of His people. Thank you so very, very, very much. I am overwhelmed with joy I can't explain.

I am praying for you and the church, always. May you be strengthened with all power, according to His glorious might, for all endurance and patience with joy, giving thanks to the Father, who has qualified you to share in the inheritance of the saints in light. Colossians 1:11–12.

In Christ, Aaron

Aaron let me know that he was praying for me and told me the contents of his prayer. He prayed Paul's prayer from the beginning of Colossians for me. What a glorious prayer indeed! Consider how much your life and the lives of others would be transformed if each of us made a regular practice to pray for people and then let them know what we prayed.

My favorite example of this in my life is a letter Gloria handed to me on the day we both graduated from seminary. I had started seminary four weeks before our wedding day, and on that first day she wrote me a prayer for my time in seminary. She kept it hidden from me for five years and then handed it to me right before the graduation ceremony and asked me to read it after I was seated. My eyes filled with tears as I read and recounted in her prayers God's faithfulness in those past five years. It was a rocky road, but

God had faithfully preserved us. We were often without money and needed God's miraculous provision. My arm ailment got so bad that during the last year I could no longer type anything. My wife had to sit and listen to me recite the content of my master's thesis and type as I spoke. Reading Gloria's prayers for me reminded me of God's steadfast love for us in preserving us through this difficult time.

The apostle Paul was amazing at this. Consider the encouragement the Philippian church received from Paul when he wrote them and told them how he prayed for them:

> I thank my God in all my remembrance of you, always in every prayer of mine for you all making my prayer with joy, because of your partnership in the gospel from the first day until now. And I am sure of this, that he who began a good work in you will bring it to completion at the day of Jesus Christ. It is right for me to feel this way about you all, because I hold you in my heart, for you are all partakers with me of grace, both in my imprisonment and in the defense and confirmation of the gospel. For God is my witness, how I yearn for you all with the affection of Christ Jesus. And it is my prayer that your love may abound more and more, with knowledge and all discernment, so that you may approve what is excellent, and so be pure and blameless for the day of Christ, filled with the fruit of righteousness that comes through Jesus Christ, to the glory and praise of God. (Phil. 1:3–11)

There's something especially sweet and encouraging about hearing the contents of someone's prayer for you. The Philippians must have been overcome with joy to hear that Paul was praying for their love to abound more and more. If that's not an encouragement to love more, I don't know what is!

It's important and helpful to pray Scripture-based prayers for our friends. In this prayer for the Philippians, Paul is not merely praying for present comfort, but that they would be ready for the future reality of Christ's return. And when he does pray for the present, he prays at the end of the prayer that they be filled with the fruit of righteousness. He's praying that fruit would result from their relationship with God. This prayer reminds us of the fruit of the Spirit listed by Paul in Galatians 5:22: love, joy, peace, patience, kindness, goodness, faithfulness, gentleness, and self-control. Paul's prayer for the Philippians is a prayer of epic proportions. Paul is praying that the Philippians would live a holy life—not that they could be perfect on this earth, but that they grow to be more like Christ each day, knowing that someday they would stand before God at the judgment seat of Christ. Incredible!

Keep praying for your friends, share with them what you're praying for, pray biblical prayers, and pray persistently. Keep praying even when it seems like nothing is happening. God can make the sun stand still, he can heal your friend, and he can grow your friend in Christlikeness.

Encourage the Hurting to Pray

We want to encourage our hurting friends and family to not stop asking God to intervene in their lives. When times are difficult, it will be tempting for them to spend more time worrying than time in prayer. We should urge them to persevere in prayer because God is with them as they pray. Numerous Scripture references illustrate this truth:

> The LORD is near to all who call on him, to all who call on him in truth. (Ps. 145:18)

> Do not be anxious about anything, but in everything by prayer and supplication with thanksgiving let your requests be made known to God. And the peace of God, which surpasses all understanding, will guard your hearts and your minds in Christ Jesus. (Phil. 4:6–7)

> Continue steadfastly in prayer, being watchful in it with thanksgiving. (Col. 4:2)

This doesn't mean God will definitely answer our prayers in the way we want him to. God is not a genie in a bottle where our wish or prayer is his command. Sometimes we pray and healing doesn't come. Your friend might ask for the darkness of depression to lift from his heart only to wake up the next morning to the same discouragement. Paul begs God to heal him of the thorn in his flesh, but God doesn't do it. God says, "My grace is sufficient for you" (2 Cor. 12:9). At the pool in Bethsaida we see Jesus walk into a huge multitude of invalids, and he heals only one. God doesn't always heal when we ask, but God in his sovereign grace has chosen to move through the prayers of his people. Prayer is God's chosen means to work in the lives of his sons and daughters, and we need to encourage our friends to press on in prayer.

We should also prompt our hurting friends to pray for perseverance in their trials. We should urge them to pray for an increased holiness as they navigate the hardships in their lives. It may or may not be God's will for them to be healed in this life, but we know for certain that it is God's will for them to grow in holiness. Paul shares this truth in his first letter to the Thessalonians, "For this is the will of God, your sanctification" (1 Thess. 4:3). It is clear: God's will for our lives is that we may be sanctified. His goal for us is that we may look more and more like Christ. Let's be certain to remind our hurting friends to humbly accept this as God's will for their lives even as we pray for healing. There is no disparity between asking for healing and praying for sanctification.

Don't stop urging your friends to pray for healing and for their souls. I know firsthand that in the midst of suffering and darkness it's easy to forgo the supernatural and despair in present circumstances. It seems counterintuitive, and yet for some reason it is easier in those moments to live in anxiety rather than run to Jesus. The power of God in prayer is the very truth I needed to hear that night at the pastor's conference. I may not remember what the pastor preached that night, but I remember the gentle encouragement from Becky to pray.

7

Hope for the Hard Conversations

My wife and I like to joke that we've known our friends Brady and Amber since we were babies. Technically, we all met in college when three out of four of us became Christians. So, we were "babes in Christ" who grew up together in our local church. We have a fun history together of traveling the world for ministry, and we even worked on plans to move overseas together after an epic road trip in southern Spain.

Several years ago Brady and Amber traveled two hours from their home to talk to Gloria and me. I can still feel the tension in the room, and I can recall exactly where I was sitting and what I was feeling. Our friends started by telling us their concern for both our marriage and our ministry. I quickly realized this wasn't a "feel good" kind of dinner with friends, laughing about the good ol' days. Brady pointed out that I was being selfish and treating Gloria poorly by blaming her for the physical pain in my arms. He rebuked me for being angry and mean to her. They told Gloria that even though she was being unjustly treated, if she didn't cut out the bitter roots in her heart, then the bitterness would begin to characterize her life. If things didn't change, our friends said, our marriage was going to end in disaster. The conversation ended with Brady and Amber saying that they loved us and were praying for us to persevere in our faith.

It was like a ton of bricks had been unloaded on top of us. We were weeks away from launching the church that we had worked for years to start. All the fundraising, relationship building, cross-cultural training, the selling of all of our stuff in the United States, and time spent church planting were flashing before our eyes. In a few days time we would host our first launch team meeting that we had given all our energy to planning.

That conversation was one of the hardest moments of my life, and yet I am eternally grateful for it. Even though the rebuke was difficult to hear, our friends were absolutely right. God used that moment to show me my sin. He had prepared me for that conversation. I was ready for it, and by his grace I quickly saw my offense for what it was—an offense not just against my wife but against the God of the universe.

I'm so thankful for our friends. Even though it wasn't easy, they chose to uphold God's values despite the potential awkwardness in our friendship. They loved us more than they loved their own comfort. What if we hadn't responded well? That possibility didn't stop their willingness to be used by God in that moment. Their loving rebuke was a starting place for repentance and transformation in our lives.

When you are caring for the hurting, it is inevitable that their circumstances will bring out their sin. Difficult trials are ripe opportunities for selfishness to come out from our hearts into the light. One of the best ways you can serve the hurting is to lovingly and carefully rebuke them by pointing out their sin and pointing them to Christ. In this chapter I'll explore some ways to be wise and tender in talking about sin issues with your friends and family who are in pain.

Rebuke Isn't Easy

Rebuke is never an easy thing to do and is something that we often run from. However, in the context of emotional pain, physical suffering, depression, loss, and tragedy, rebuke is something you may *have* to do. As Christians, we understand that repentance is to be our way of life, and as much as rebuke is difficult, we need it. Suffering loss and experiencing pain often trigger an eruption of the sinfulness of our hearts. While being gentle with the hurting is key, at times (like with our friends Brady and Amber) you will need to prayerfully discern how and when to bring up issues in their lives. This is not something to take lightly, but it's for their good and the glory of God. He has sovereignly placed you in their life to help them grow in Christlikeness. In fact, nothing can be more loving than the rebuke that brings a fellow believer back from the path of sin. Bonhoeffer says, "It is a ministry of mercy, an ultimate offer of genuine fellowship, when we allow nothing but God's word to stand between us."[1]

The apostle Paul certainly didn't revel in rebuking people, but he modeled it well for us. He wrote in the book of Galatians about a specific occasion when he rebuked another believer in his hometown. The other Christian was none other than the apostle Peter whom Paul noticed was living in hypocrisy and dragging others down with him. Paul approached Peter publicly in what has to be one of the more tense and awkward episodes in the New Testament. This particular confrontation takes place right in the middle of the church picnic. This is supposed to be a time of sweet fellowship and celebration, right? But in this case, what happened was the equivalent of one pastor getting on the megaphone to publicly rebuke another pastor during a fellowship dinner.

Paul, the apostle, rebukes Peter the apostle. These were Christians, forgiven through Christ, apostles of Christ, honored in the churches for their leadership, doing great things for God, being used mightily by God, and Paul rebukes Peter. Why? Galatians 2 tells us what happened:

> But when Cephas (Peter) came to Antioch, I opposed him to his face, because he stood condemned. For before certain men came from James, he was eating with the Gentiles; but when they came he drew back and separated himself, fearing the circumcision party. And the rest of the Jews acted hypocritically along with him, so that even Barnabas was led astray by their hypocrisy. But when I saw that their conduct was not in step with the truth of the gospel, I said to Cephas before them all, "If you, though a Jew, live like a Gentile and not like a Jew, how can you force the Gentiles to live like Jews?" (vv. 11–14)

Paul rebuked Peter because Peter changed his eating habits and stopped eating with the Gentiles. This might not seem like a very important issue, but we need to remember that in ancient times eating was a significant cultural event. Eating with someone was considered a big deal and was a sacred time between people. This is why people were outraged when Jesus ate with tax collectors and sinners. The Old Testament laws stated that you couldn't eat unclean foods or eat in the presence of those who were unclean.

God had already sent Peter a vision to show him that the ceremonial law was finished. In the vision, Peter saw a sheet full of the animals forbidden to him in the Old Testament law and heard a voice saying, "Kill and eat.... What God has made clean, do not call common" (Acts 10:13, 15). God had already made it clear to Peter that the cleanliness laws have been fulfilled in Christ and that he could sit with the Gentiles and eat with them. He had already seen true-life examples that God accepts men from every ethnicity, and he began to sit and eat bacon cheeseburgers and lobster with Tom and Padmini and Philip and Joanna and Nisin and Jason and Lucia and Donita. However, Peter reverted to his original eating habits right before everyone's eyes, ignoring what God had taught him about completion of the ceremonial law, so Paul rebuked him in front of everyone for his hypocrisy.

While it sounds harsh, this is the most loving thing Paul could have done for Peter and the other believers who witnessed the incident. If Paul had not rebuked Peter, this gospel issue would have split the church, and today we'd have a Jewish branch of Christianity and a Gentile branch. The text says that the split was already under way as many of the Jews and even Barnabas were led astray by Peter's hypocrisy (Gal. 2:13).

None of us live alone on an island. Our sin and hypocrisy shape our family life, our friends, our small group, and our church. Our private and secret sins affect others, even if we do not see the immediate effects of them. A pornography addiction affects our marriage. Idleness and laziness hurt our coworkers. Our anger problem distresses our children. Greed and stinginess hinder the church's ministry. Our response to pain and suffering can drastically affect strangers, too.

In the instance in Galatia, Paul told Peter that racism is not in line with the gospel. Racism is forgetting you are saved by Jesus's blood—not your blood. Peter had betrayed the truth that God doesn't treat us on the basis of race but saves us by grace alone. His behavior was undermining his belief. People were watching, and it didn't matter what he said, because he wasn't living in line with the truth of the gospel.

Rebuke, when done right, can be life-changing. This could not have been easy for Paul, but nothing short of the glory of Christ was at stake. If we are honest, we are faced with similar situations and are tempted to keep quiet. We often hesitate to rebuke others because we are keenly conscious of our own sins. We know that the finger could be pointed right back at us, and we know we should take the log out of our own eyes before pointing out the speck in another's eye (Matt. 7:3–5). We also realize we should not rebuke in a temper tantrum or unrighteous anger. Other times we stay quiet because we are lazy, or we don't want to create division among friends. We are afraid that confrontation may ruin a good friendship. Bonhoeffer is again helpful here:

> Why should we be afraid of one another, since both of us have only God to fear? Why should we think that our brother would not understand us, when we understood very well what was meant when somebody spoke God's comfort or God's admonition to us, perhaps in words that were halting and unskilled? Or do we really think there is a single person in this world who does not need either encouragement or admonition? Why, then, has God bestowed Christian brotherhood upon us?[2]

I'm thankful that Paul stepped up to rebuke Peter. He loved the Galatians enough to warn them sternly and to plead with them personally, and he cared more for their souls than whether they would like him. Eternal joy mattered more to Paul than temporary, earthly happiness.

I'm also thankful that my friends Brady and Amber stepped up to rebuke me a couple of months before we started the church. A true friend is the one who tells the truth even when it is difficult. Brady and Amber's rebuke showed me that they truly loved me and valued our friendship, and their example of cherishing God's glory more than anything else still speaks to me today. Our friendship was only strengthened after their gracious rebuke.

Reorienting Worship

Loving rebuke can be a life-changing event that moves people from worshiping themselves to properly worshiping the Savior. In reality the goal is the same as counseling believers to work through struggles in their life. Jeremy Pierre and Deepak Reju describe counseling in this way: "Counseling is not primarily an attempt to fix problems, but is an attempt to reorient worship from created things to the Creator by means of the gospel of Jesus Christ."[3] The goal of counseling is not simply to provide specific guidance for the person's problems but to uncover what his heart is worshiping and to offer redemptive remedies for his struggles.[4] Counseling announces the truth of the gospel with the hope that the person will turn from sin and cling to Christ. This is our hope as we have hard conversations. We want to see our friends turn from worshiping one thing to worshiping Christ. As people are pressed due to their pain or loss, they will be tempted to turn to things apart from Christ. A true friend will, at the right time, gently and prayerfully speak into that person's life to see what he or she is worshiping. You will ask heart-penetrating questions appropriately. Here are some lightly adapted "X-ray questions" that counselor David Powlison finds helpful in dealing with concerns of the heart:

- Where do you bank your hopes? People energetically sacrifice to attain what they hope for. What is it? People in despair have had hopes dashed. What were those shattered hopes?
- What do you fear? What do you not want? What do you tend to worry about? Sinful fears invert cravings. If I want to avoid something at all costs—loss of reputation, loss of control, poverty, ill health, rejection, etc.—I am ruled by a lustful fear.
- What do you think you need? What are your "felt needs"? Felt needs often masquerade as self-evident necessities to be acquired, not as deceptive slave-masters. Our culture of need reinforces the flesh's instincts and habits. In most cases, a person's felt needs are street talk for idolatrous demands for love, understanding, a sense of being in control, affirmation, and achievement.

- Where do you find refuge, safety, comfort, escape, pleasure, or security? You must dig out your false trusts and your escapisms that substitute for the Lord. Many "addictive behaviors" are helpfully brought to light when we ask this question. They often arise in the context of life's troubles and pressures, and function as false refuges.

- Whom must you please? Whose opinion of you counts? From whom do you desire approval and fear rejection? Whose value system do you measure yourself against? In whose eyes are you living? Whose love and approval do you need?

- How do you define and weigh success and failure, right and wrong, desirable and undesirable, in any particular situation?

- What do you pray for? Your prayers often reveal the pattern of your imbalance and self-centeredness. Of the many possible things to ask for, what do you concentrate on? Prayer is about desire; we ask for what we want. Do your prayers reflect the desires of God or of the flesh?

- What do you think about most often? What preoccupies or obsesses you? What is the first thing your mind turns to when you wake up in the morning?

- Where do you find your identity? How do you define who you are?[5]

Asking questions like these will help unveil what's happening in your friend's heart. The goal in your counseling-type conversations is to help your friends consider what it is they are worshiping. You're not trying to apply a quick fix to their problems but to help them see what's already going on in their heart. By taking them to God's Word, you can help them line up their lives with the truth. It's important to take people to God's Word so they see what *God* has to say about the situation rather than simply rely on your words.

Condoning and Condemning

In the area of rebuking others and speaking hard truths into their lives, we tend to fluctuate between two extremes. On the one hand we tend to condone the sin by staying silent. We say, *Sure, they're having problems, but doesn't the Bible say: "Judge not, lest you be judged"? So, nothing I can do. I can't judge so I just need to let it go.* However, in Matthew 7:1 Jesus wasn't saying, "Don't judge"; he was saying don't judge *unless* you're willing for God to call you to the same standard in your life. That verse doesn't mean you can't confront someone in sin. Hebrews 10 gives us a good picture of what happens if we don't confront someone who is in sin:

> For if we go on sinning deliberately after receiving the knowledge of the truth, there no longer remains a sacrifice for sins, but a fearful expectation of judgment, and a fury of fire that will consume the adversaries. Anyone who has set aside the law of Moses dies without mercy on the evidence of two or three witnesses. How much worse punishment, do you think, will be deserved by the one who has trampled underfoot the Son of God, and has profaned the blood of the covenant by which he was sanctified, and has outraged the Spirit of grace? For we know him who said, "Vengeance is mine; I will repay." And again, "The Lord will judge his people." It is a fearful thing to fall into the hands of the living God. (Heb. 10:26–31)

Condoning sin isn't gentleness. No, it is pure selfishness, because you're not willing to love your brother and sister by selflessly speaking about the gospel with them. It only leads to further judgment. Souls are at stake. For their good and God's glory you must pursue them and speak the truth in love.

It is also possible to go to the opposite extreme and condemn harshly. When we do that, we look down on others and judge them without extending the hand of grace. Instead of reminding them where forgiveness can be found, we only point them to judgment. We can also turn confrontation into gossip as we spread the information of someone's sin in the disguise of a prayer request. "Oh, I just wish you would pray with me about Brian. God bless his soul." "Oh friend, we've got to pray for Joanne. Did you see what she did this weekend? I did some detective work on her Facebook page. Go look and see for yourself."

We can easily fall into extremes by either condoning sin by our silence or condemning the sinner in harshness or gossip. Paul instructs us on how to confront correctly: "Brothers, if anyone is caught in any transgression, you who are spiritual should restore him in a spirit of gentleness. Keep watch on yourself, lest you too be tempted" (Gal. 6:1).

Paul instructs the believers in Galatia on how to restore one caught in sin. He offers an explanation of what he has just modeled in confronting Peter. It's not right to condone or condemn sinners but instead to confront them in gentleness and compassion with the hope of restoration.

The word *restore* is used in medical practice to describe putting a bone back in joint in order to make a dysfunctional bone functional again.[6] When you confront and restore someone, Paul says you must do two things. First, you maintain a spirit of gentleness. This balance of truth-plus-love is crucial. As Pastor Tim Chester writes, "Love without truth is like doing heart surgery with a wet fish. But truth without love is like doing heart surgery with a hammer."[7] We must embody truth, not just express it. Truth infused with love is incarnated in our lives as we live it out with one another. Second, Paul says to keep watch on yourself. When confronting sin, we might be tempted to rejoice in it and let arrogance consume us. We might consider ourselves in light of that other person, and say to ourselves, "Wow, she is bad off. I am glad I'm not like her. Oh, yes, of course I have other sins, but I would never fall for that one."

A friend of mine came back from a rain forest tour in Central America and told me that at one point the tour guide said to be careful while walking, because the jungle was full of jaguars. The tour group was urged to stay on the path and not wander off alone. My friend turned to the guy next to him and asked, "Can you outrun a jaguar?" The man replied with a chuckle, "I don't have to outrun a jaguar, I just have to outrun you." That's a funny story, but in reality that's how we often think about ourselves. It's easy for us to become arrogant or conceited by thinking we're better than someone else. We need to watch our pride when we think we don't have the same sin struggles as our brothers or sisters. They are not the standard, God is.

If you're not careful, it's also easy to become a sin sleuth—a person that specializes in seeing everyone else's problems. Eventually all of your kids, your spouse, the elders at your church, your bosses, your coworkers, and everyone else has a sin problem. *Everyone . . . except you.* You can rattle off a list of their transgressions without even thinking. Have you noticed the common denominator in all those relationships? It's you. We need to be careful that we don't start noticing the specks in everyone else's eyes when all the while we have a huge log in our own eye. Keep a close watch on your life and work hard to acknowledge the sin in your own life so that you will have a safeguard from condoning or condemning your friend's sin.

Two Final Considerations

There are two more questions in Galatians 6:1. The first is, When do you confront someone? Notice Paul doesn't say, *Confront someone every time you get the chance.* Discerning *when* confrontation is needed certainly takes some wisdom. Paul's letter doesn't say

every time you see someone sin, seek to restore him. This is helpful because if you're ministering to someone who is undergoing
tremendous pain and suffering, he might be dealing with many rec-
ognizable sins. Instead, the verse says to confront if someone is
caught in a sin. It seems like Paul is referring to someone who is
deceived by his sin. This sort of sin is a regular occurrence, and
the person hasn't recognized or repented of it yet. Perhaps he is
struggling with a sin that has overtaken him by surprise, and he is
blinded by it. If he recognizes his sin and he's working on it, the text
seems to imply that you don't have to confront him. Don't berate
him with it. If he's open about it, you don't need to convene a meeting to deal with it. In my case, Brady and Amber had seen a pattern of repeated sin on my part and that my heart was hardened to
the truth. Time went on, and I wasn't making any changes or even
acknowledging that it was my fault. I needed to be lovingly rebuked
for the sin that I was blinded to.

Another question that Paul answers for us is, Who should do the
confronting? Paul says, "You who are spiritual." This doesn't mean
that we leave the rebuking to the experts. You can't say that because
you've only been a Christian for a few years, you're not ready to confront someone yet. That's not at all what Paul is saying in this verse.
Paul is saying that you with the "Spirit" should restore a brother. It's
not Paul's way of saying, "Leave it to an 'advanced' group of Christians." (There is no such thing.) He's actually making a point to say
the opposite. He's saying, "Christian, you with the Spirit should go
seek to restore that person." Clearly it's wise that the one seeking
to restore be someone walking by the Spirit, led by the Spirit, and
seeking to keep in step with the Spirit, but there aren't different
classes of Christians. There's no caste system within Christianity.
All Christians walking with God should be open and able to do this.

Some might argue that one's relationship with the Lord is a private matter. That we need to let God deal with others and not med-

dle in another person's affairs. However, we never encounter this "private" relationship language in Scripture. It doesn't exist. We do have what Paul Tripp calls "intentionally intrusive relationships" commanded in Scripture.[8] The book of Proverbs speaks to this in a number of different places:

> Faithful are the wounds of a friend; profuse are the kisses of an enemy. (Prov. 27:6)

> Iron sharpens iron, and one man sharpens another. (Prov. 27:17)

Ask yourself how you are handling hard conversations with your hurting friends. Are you intentionally speaking the truth of God's Word in love to them? Are you gently looking for ways to point them to Christ in the midst of their sinful responses? Do you have eternity in mind when you think of your relationships? Are you willing to speak hard truths to others if it means it will rescue them from danger? Are you more worried about your comfort, and you don't want to jeopardize your comfortable relationship? You have to ask yourself the question, Do I value that person's soul more than my friendship with him?

People suffering with pain, depression, or loss will be pressed in ways they've never been pressed before. Naturally, their sin will show itself. It's not an excuse, but they will need faithful friends who will be committed to the well-being of their souls by rebuking them in love. Help your friends know that they need to stay in community and that the cross has already criticized them more than anyone else can. It took the violent, unjust death of the perfect Son of God to atone for their vile wickedness. Because of the cross, we all have the freedom to stand up and be honest that our lives aren't perfect. Jesus's death on the cross is the only proof we need to remind ourselves that we can't be perfect.

I don't know where I'd be today if Brady and Amber hadn't loved me enough to sit me down and share their concerns about my sin. In that moment God used the faithful wounds of friends to lift me out of that dark tunnel and point me to Christ. I repented and relied on Christ to change my life. And he did.

8

Whatever You Do, Don't Do These Things

If you ever fly with me on an airplane, you'll see that I can't keep my eyes from staring outside during takeoff and landing. I love the views of cities, oceans, and mountains that you get from the plane. Even though I've traveled out of the Dubai airport countless times over the years, I can't help but stare with the curiosity of a little child as we fly by the world's tallest building and other fun landmarks in our great city.

I must admit, however, that after I read an article that said most plane crashes happen at takeoff or landing, I've been just a little anxious at the beginning and end of my flights. I may be looking out the window with curious eyes, but I am also asking God for protection in those moments of the flight. It reminds me of a story about an airplane that barely survived a crash landing when it landed at the wrong airport. The pilots were landing in a small city in the United States and accidentally touched down at a much smaller private airport seven miles away from their intended destination. During their approach, the pilots were in contact with the control tower and were told that they were fifteen miles away from their target. They responded that they actually had their target in sight and were going to land.

Upon landing, the pilots had to stomp on the breaks extra hard to avoid going over a ledge, and they nearly crashed the plane. Passengers later described the landing as mayhem and that the air was filled with the stench of burnt rubber. The pilots admitted to being shocked at the mistake and told investigators that they saw the bright lights of an airport in front of them and so they landed there. They honestly thought it was the right airport.[1]

How crazy is that story? The pilots thought they knew better than the instruments on their plane and the air traffic controllers on the ground. They saw an airport in the distance and thought, "Hey, we're here. Let's go ahead and land. It looks like an airport. It must be the right one." But it doesn't matter how sincere you are in landing a plane if you're landing in the wrong place.

The same goes for taking care of those experiencing pain and suffering. You may think you have the right approach and goal in caring for your friend going through depression, your sick elderly mother, a couple struggling through miscarriage, or a friend grieving the loss of a career, but it doesn't matter how sincere you are if you are way off target. I have experienced many well-meaning individuals who had good intentions but at the end of the day only exacerbated my hurt. And sometimes I thought I was doing good for someone else when I was actually causing more pain. In our sincerity we can still be wrong! We need God's help to care for our friends who are distressed.

In this chapter I discuss ten approaches to caring for the hurting that look helpful on the surface, but in the end may only add to the pain. I'll start each section with a brief quote of what someone using this approach might actually say to someone. You could title this section "The Ten Commandments of What Not to Do for Your

Hurting Friend." In the end, I hope you'll see that God's love triumphs in your weaknesses. We don't know the answers, and we can't fix things, but he is faithful to care for our friends *in the midst* of their pain.

1. Don't Be the Fix-It Person

"I've been thinking about you. I've picked up this brand-new organic, all-natural ointment that will surely heal your disability. My grandmother used it for her foot pain, and it went away in a week. It should heal you too!"

The truth is, nobody wants another treatment, ointment, acupuncture reference, or diet that is 100 percent guaranteed to get their hopes up higher than they've ever been before.

I can't tell you how many times I've been handed another bag full of exotic creams in some language I couldn't understand. I can't count the number of times people have given me something that they claim has healed someone with the same ailment that I have. When you make these claims and guarantee healing, it may highlight to the one who is hurting that you have no idea what kind of issues they are actually dealing with. Many times people hand me something like a bar of soap blessed by a "holy man," saying it's going to heal me, but all that really shows is that they have no idea how much pain I'm going through. They don't understand that my nerves are completely mangled and not working. Now, it's entirely possible that God could miraculously heal me through a smelling salt or an herbal tea, but that's not the normal prescription for nerves that don't work.

Struggling people have probably already seen numerous doctors and undergone different treatments. Unless they are sitting around and not doing anything, they have people with actual medical degrees who are looking into their situation. It's in our nature to want to offer a solution for a problem. And that's great! We yearn to help and often have great intentions by wanting to fix things. The heart behind this is generally wonderful, but sometimes the best help is a listening ear to the problems that a person is really facing. Proverbs 10:19 says, "When words are many, transgression is not lacking, but whoever restrains his lips is prudent." A better approach would be to ask more questions and grow in your understanding of another's pain rather than offering solutions for something you know very little about. Sometimes the best thing you can do is say, "I'm sorry, can you help me better understand what you are going through?" And then listen.

2. Don't Play the Comparison Game

"Oh, wow, you have arm pain. I had tennis elbow one time, and it was really rough. I couldn't play any sports for a couple of weeks. I know exactly what you're going through."

Unless you're Jesus, it almost never helps to tell someone that you know *exactly* what he or she is going through. If you've gone through the horrendous thing your friend or family member is going through, then surely they know it. We think we're encouraging others by proclaiming we've gone through something similar, when in reality what they're going through may be much different from our past experience. It is certainly not exactly the same.

Another way you might play the comparison game is to point out other people who have it worse than your friend. We might think we're helping when we tell someone who has a hurt leg, "Well, at least you still have a leg. There are thousands of people around the world who don't have any legs, and they can't walk at all. Praise God for the leg you have!" But how is that supposed to make the person feel? Not better, that's for sure. Don't start your "encouragement" by saying, "Chin up, it's not as bad as that time when I . . ." or "This reminds me of the day when I . . ." When you do this, you minimize another person's suffering. You are making your suffering friend feel like his pain is "no big deal." To people in pain—whatever their issue is—it is a big deal. A person's suffering is no small suffering to that person in that moment. If you minimize a person's pain, it will compound his hurt even more. And when a person's experience of his real pain is invalidated, then he is not pointed to Christ for hope and help. Why bother Jesus with something that's really no big deal?

It's also best to not start any sentence with the words "at least." "At least she died when she was young." "At least she's in heaven now." "At least you have three other children." "At least your mind is still strong." "At least you have a great family." A better way forward is to say, "I love you" and "I am so sorry," and to pour out your heart in compassion for the one hurting because what he's going through is difficult and unique to him.

Rather than working hard to remember your distant relative who went through something similar and sharing those stories, show sympathy and love for the hurting person *who is right in front of you*. Instead of comparing your friend to someone you know, you might say, "I don't pretend to understand what you're going through, but I want to try. Help me understand how you are feeling." If you find it difficult to sympathize, Paul tells us in 2 Corinthians that we can comfort someone not because we can relate to them but because Christ can relate to us.

> Blessed be the God and Father of our Lord Jesus Christ, the Father of mercies and God of all comfort, who comforts us in all our affliction, so that we may be able to comfort those who are in any affliction, with the comfort with which we ourselves are comforted by God. For as we share abundantly in Christ's sufferings, so through Christ we share abundantly in comfort too. If we are afflicted, it is for your comfort and salvation; and if we are comforted, it is for your comfort, which you experience when you patiently endure the same sufferings that

we suffer. Our hope for you is unshaken, for we know that as you share in our sufferings, you will also share in our comfort. (2 Cor. 1:3–7)

Because Christ comforts us in our affliction (whatever it may be), we can then go out and comfort others in whatever they are going through without having gone through the exact same problem.

3. Don't Make It Their Identity

"Hi, nice to see you. How's your back? Is it feeling any better? Have you gotten any rest? Are you in a lot of pain right now? How is it compared to how you were last week? You really don't look very good right now, maybe you should sit down."

Another of the ten commandments of what not to do for your hurting friends is to bring up their pain so much that it becomes their identity. If you talk about it all the time, you are at risk of defining them by their struggle and pain as if that's all they're about. We need to be careful to not constantly bring up their suffering. At the same time, we want to show we care, so this is a tough balance to keep. As you care for your friend, it is important to remember that if your friend has a disability, he is not fundamentally a disabled person. If he is a Christian, then he is a Christian who has a disability. If your friend has lost his job, he is not fundamentally an unemployed person. If he is a Christian, then he is a Christian who is unemployed. As a Christian, his primary identity is as a son of the living God. He is a human being who has an immortal soul, redeemed out of the kingdom of darkness. In "The Weight of Glory," C. S. Lewis reminds us that there are no ordinary people. He says,

> You have never talked to a mere mortal. Nations, cultures, arts, civilizations—these are mortal, and their life is to ours as the life of a gnat. But it is immortals whom we joke with, work with,

marry, snub, and exploit—immortal horrors or everlasting splendors.[2]

The apostle Paul understands this truth but goes even further and says that the fundamental identity of Christians is that they are in Christ. That despite our sin and wickedness, God did the following:

> But God, being rich in mercy, because of the great love with which he loved us, even when we were dead in our trespasses, made us alive together with Christ—by grace you have been saved—and raised us up with him and seated us with him in the heavenly places in Christ Jesus, so that in the coming ages he might show the immeasurable riches of his grace in kindness toward us in Christ Jesus. (Eph. 2:4–7)

A believer now lives in light of a completely new reality. Our sinful condition is reversed. New Testament scholar Peter O'Brien points out that the origins of God's saving work are found in his mercy (v. 4), his great love (v. 4), his rich grace (vv. 5, 7, and 8), and his kindness to us in Christ Jesus (v. 7). O'Brien writes that "the whole paragraph [in Ephesians] emphasizes that God acted on our behalf simply because of his own gracious and merciful character."[3] We have gone from being enemies of God to being "in Christ" (v. 7). This is the reality for the Christian. Now that we are saved by grace, God views believers as he views his Son. This is remarkable. When God the Father looks at us, he sees Jesus. When he looks at a Christian who has a disability, he doesn't primarily see disability; above all he sees his Son. When he looks at a Christian who is weak or sick, he doesn't see sickness but our Savior.

As we interact with believers who are hurting, realize that their identity is that of being in Christ Jesus. When you speak to them, help them draw their gaze to Christ so they can see things from an eternal perspective, and consistently remind them that their identity is not in their circumstances, but in their Savior.

4. Don't Promise Deliverance Now

"Oh, I just know you are going to get healed. You love Jesus and are faithful to him so he will definitely heal you. Just be patient and think positive and keep the faith and you'll be healed in no time at all."

When we 100 percent guarantee that God will deliver our friends from their suffering in this earthly life, we make God out to be some type of cosmic vending machine. Your prayer requests become command central for getting God to do the exact thing you want when you want it. This is embodied in the health-and-wealth prosperity gospel that is destroying churches and lives around the world. It teaches that you should tithe more so you'll get more. It encourages you to serve in ministry more so God will bless you in the workplace. And it tells you to live a moral life so God can pay you back what he owes you for being so good. The problem with this false gospel is that God can never be put in our debt. God never owes us anything.

The gospel is not a message that with Jesus you'll get rich or be successful, or that if you follow Christ, you'll be happy, healthy, wealthy, and wise. That message has more to do with Happy Meals than Jesus's call to his disciples to take up their crosses and follow him. When you give the promise of healing to the hurting, you inevitably overpromise and underdeliver. Eventually this message lets you down. If you see God as a vending machine, then you will become disillusioned when your candy bar doesn't drop after payment has been submitted. When you promise healing for your friend, he will be crushed if it doesn't happen.

Instead of promising deliverance, remind them of the presence of God. A Christian worships God for God, because God is more precious than anything this world has to offer. God is the beginning and the end. He's the goal—more of him, not more of the stuff you think you can get from him. The prosperity gospel is basically what Martin Luther called a false theology of glory. That is, the belief that if you follow these instructions, then God will give you happiness.[4] God becomes a buddy or a partner who exists to serve your needs. Salvation becomes not a matter of divine rescue from the judgment that is coming on the world but rather a matter of self-improvement in order to have your best life here and now. It twists the truth because Christ came not to bring earthly happiness but to save us from death and judgment, and he did so through suffering. Jesus says in John 12 in reference to the cross, "But for this purpose I have come" (v. 27). And in Luke 19, "The Son of Man came to seek and to save the lost" (v. 10).

Over the past decade or so, various well-meaning people have kindly told me that God was going to heal me. They have tried to encourage me that since I am a man of faith and I love God, I'll be healed. Some have said that because I am a pastor and am doing the Lord's work, I will be healed. Many have said that God would bless my faithfulness by giving me good health. Others have said, "It's all going to be okay." Now, they're right and they're wrong. God will one day heal me, but it might not come here on earth. I may never get to pick up my baby in this life. However, in the next, I will not shed another tear as I ponder whether I will ever be able to play ball with my sons. In this life I may not be able to button my shirt and put on my shoes by myself, but in the next life I will be perfectly dressed in Christ's righteousness. Instead of promising deliverance in this life, point them to God's presence and a future hope that will never let them down.

5. Don't Encourage Them to Just "Move On"

"Don't be sad; you should be happy because they're better off in heaven with Jesus anyway. That's a much better place to be, so it would be best for you to move on with your life."

We never want to give the impression that a person's pain or sorrow doesn't matter, or that people should just gird up their loins and get on with life. When we disregard their earthly pain and only point them to their heavenly reward, we fail to comfort them *in their pain*.

It's also unhelpful to tell people (or show it by your nonverbal actions) that it is high time they got over the grief of life in a fallen world, because you are tired of being reminded of their suffering. The pressure to "get over it" typically increases the pain of the one grieving. Instead, tell them it is okay to grieve and weep. As we saw earlier in the book, a number of psalms of lament reveal that the writers are openly grieving to God. They are filled with cries of pain and heartache. Encourage your friend to be honest about his emotions and get them all out on the table. Christians have the propensity to force a trivial kind of mandatory happiness in the church. Telling someone to get back to his "normal" life is of no help, because his life will never be the same. If he lost his mother, he will never have his mother again on this earth.

Jesus did not dismiss others when they looked like a bruised reed beyond repair. In fact, Jesus himself experienced our grief: "He was despised and rejected by men; a man of sorrows, and acquainted with grief; and as one from whom men hide their faces he was despised, and we esteemed him not" (Isa. 53:3). Jesus was "acquainted with grief" and is not unable to sympathize with our weaknesses. Hebrews 4:14–16 says,

> Since then we have a great high priest who has passed through the heavens, Jesus, the Son of God, let us hold fast our confession. For we do not have a high priest who is unable to sympathize with our weaknesses, but one who in every respect has been tempted as we are, yet without sin. Let us then with confidence draw near to the throne of grace, that we may receive mercy and find grace to help in time of need.

Jesus has experienced your friend's grief and identifies with him in his pain. Jesus loves him and is able to supply all that he needs to persevere to the end. Suffering people need to be able to weep and pour out their hearts and not immediately be shut down by being told to move on. It's unhelpful to simply tell someone to pull himself together. Instead, listen to his struggles and pain, and let him know that Jesus is with him in his pain, for he suffered persecution, loneliness, desertion, beatings, emotional and physical abuse, crucifixion, and the wrath of God the Father. Jesus won't beat up a bruised reed, but will hold him in his arms. Let your friend grieve, and tell him it's okay to weep and have no answers. Jesus doesn't minimize pain, but rather he cares for suffering people.

6. Don't Bring on the Inquisition

"I'm sorry your husband is in the hospital because of that accident. Was he even wearing his seat belt? Do you think he was texting someone on the phone while driving?"

When friends are in a crisis or grieving, it is often helpful to ask questions and practice the art of listening. However, certain questions will do more harm than good. This is not the time to inquire whether it was "their" fault (like Job's friends did) that they are in a terrible situation or have lost a loved one. It's not the time to ask them questions like, "Were you two even that close anyway?" When you're at a loss for words, it may be best to say, "Friend, I honestly don't know what to say right now, but I want you to know that I love you."

Instead of bringing on the inquisition, another way forward is to join them and God in saying things like, "I am so sorry; death and pain and loss are absolutely terrible. Things weren't supposed to be this way. This isn't good." Instead of trying to get answers to questions, you can take the biblical advice and "rejoice with those who rejoice, weep with those who weep" (Rom. 12:15). As you weep with someone, rather than asking questions about various details that could be hurtful, a good question to ask is, "How are you doing today?" Notice I didn't just ask, "How are you doing?" If someone lost a loved one a month ago, how do you think he is doing? Pretty lousy, probably. When you add that simple word *today*, you are acknowledging that it's an everyday battle, and he must struggle through each day. Ask questions that are going to open up someone's heart to you, not enlarge his anger or pain.

7. Don't Be Hyperspiritual

"Praise the Lord your baby has passed away. Her pain is now gone, and she is with Jesus!"

I read a real story of a real pastor who went up to a real mother who had just lost her real baby and said those words above. "Praise the Lord!" the pastor uttered. The mother was a bit stunned and said, "Excuse me?" The pastor responded, "Praise the Lord she's not in pain anymore!" The mom was shocked. She couldn't believe the insensitivity of his comment.

Another hurtful comment I've often heard people say to those suffering is, "Just wait, you will see later on how God is going to use all of this for something really good." Clichés like "oh, just pray more and everything will be great" or "turn to God and it will be all right" don't offer real encouragement in those moments. Statements like "look on the bright side" or "she's in a better place" aren't going to fill the hurting person's heart. These types of comments could even be offensive, because you're implying that the person is not praying or trusting God in those moments.

It's also wise to refrain from "playing God" in your interactions with those who are suffering. Don't try to explain what God is doing behind the scenes: "That baby was just not meant to be born." "Your sickness really is a blessing; God is preparing you for good works." "You are being spared from even worse things." The truth is you don't know the specifics of what God is doing. In his legendary words to Job, God makes it clear that we don't know the mind of God.

> Where were you when I laid the foundation of the earth?
>> Tell me, if you have understanding.
> Who determined its measurements—surely you know!
>> Or who stretched the line upon it?
> On what were its bases sunk,
>> or who laid its cornerstone,
> when the morning stars sang together
>> and all the sons of God shouted for joy? (Job 38:4–7)

Instead of trying to figure out what God is doing and get inside his mind, it's better to say things like, "I have no idea what God is doing in this situation, but I know he is holy and good." Be as bewildered by your friend's suffering as he is, and instead of providing answers from the mind of God, point him to the love of Christ who will never fail him.

8. Don't Play the Avoidance Game

After all these cautions, you may be tempted to do nothing when your friend is hurting. I sure hope that's not the case!

I haven't written an example quote of this commandment, because there is nothing to say. That's exactly what you do when you play the avoidance game. You ignore the person's pain completely. While it may not be as dramatic as saying the wrong thing at the wrong time, it can be just as hurtful.

I have often made the mistake of being unresponsive after learning that someone in our congregation lost a loved one. On one occasion I terribly hurt a couple, because I had not called them after the passing of the lady's mother. I called and profusely apologized, but the damage was done. I made it clear by my inaction that I did not care enough about them to make a simple phone call. I underestimated how much they were hurting and lost an opportunity to love and care for my fellow members.

It's also incredibly awkward to not even mention that you know that someone is grieving. It's painful when we don't acknowledge the person's loss and show sympathy. I read about a lady who went to a family reunion after her son died, and no one even said the boy's name. Apparently, they were afraid of making her cry. She later made a button that she wore that said, "When you mention my child, I may cry. If you don't mention his name, it will break my heart."[5] You might be nervous about saying something hurtful, but playing the avoidance game won't help either. Be prayerful in what you say, but don't underestimate the power of the right words at the right time. Proverbs 25:11–12 makes this point: "A word fitly spoken is like apples of gold in a setting of silver. Like a gold ring or an ornament of gold is a wise reprover to a listening ear."

After someone loses a loved one, some friends will immediately send a card or a note of sympathy but never again say anything. One way to go the extra mile is to mark down the date of the death and send a card to your friend or family member the following year, telling her that you are remembering her loss. When it's not our pain, we forget quickly, but for the one bereaved, that day will never be forgotten.

9. Don't Pledge General Help

"Oh friend, you can count on me to help you. If there is anything I can do, please let me know and I'd love to do whatever you need. Don't hesitate to call me day or night."

Let's be honest: for many of us, asking for help goes against every fiber of our being. When I'm lost, I'd rather drive around in circles than stop and ask a total stranger for directions.

When I was in New York City last year, I had one of these "I should have asked for help" kind of experiences. I had bought some new headphones at the airport, and I sat down to plug them into my phone. When I sat down, I realized that my arm disability meant I couldn't open the plastic package. I thought about going back and asking for help at the store, but I thought that would be awkward. I needed my headphones, so I did what I thought was the next best thing. I took off my shoes and stuck a pen between my toes and laid the headphone package on the ground. I then started trying to stab the container with my armed foot. Eventually, after a bit of hard work and determination and quite a few stab wounds, the package opened.

As I later processed my foot stabbing episode at JFK airport, I realized a couple of things. First, stabbing something with your foot at the airport in New York City is pretty weird and very unwise. It's not the type of place where you want to draw much attention to yourself with strange movements and stabbing sounds. I also realized that even after all these years of dealing with the nerve disease in my arms, I still have a hard time asking for help. I like to be independent. I like to be seen as strong. I prefer to do things on my own, and it's important to me to feel like I am in control.

Knowing how hard it is for people to ask for help, we need to offer assistance in a way that is easy to accept. When you pledge general help to someone in need, it's not likely that he or she will take you up on the offer. Sometimes a general offer of help just makes us feel good about ourselves. When we pledge general help, we put the burden on the hurting; we expect *them* to come up with a way for us to help. That's a tough assignment to put on someone grieving or in pain. They may not even be thinking clearly, and now they have to come up with ways that they can be helped.

We should make it easy on others to receive help by just doing something. We should not be mere hearers of the Word, but doers of the Word (James 1:22). If you really want to help a hurting friend, then offer to help in a specific way.

I have friends that have worked hard to understand my disability and have offered help that I've really needed. I joked in the introduction about one of our elders who cut my steak, but that steak-cutting is a perfect example of what I'm talking about. Mack didn't wait for me to ask; he jumped in and helped me. Figure out what you can do and, like the Nike slogan exhorts, "Just do it." If your friend likes Quarter Pounder's with cheese from McDonald's, show up at his house with an Extra Value Meal and a vanilla milk shake. If your hurting friend has lots of little kids in the house, tell her you will come over the next weekend to help with childcare, and ask her what time works best. Of course in some situations, such as a family member dying of cancer, you will want to check with a family member or close friend of the hurting and find out what would actually be helpful. In some cases, a visit may be the last thing that will help your friend in that moment.

If you are aware of a specific need, work to do it. And remember that at first people will flock to the hurting to help, but then as time goes by that help will begin to diminish. Make sure you help specifically and keep it up as time goes on. They will still need you.

10. Don't Condemn Them

"Did you know that God is punishing you right now? What might you have done that brought on this kind of suffering? Can you think of a secret sin that you've committed that God might be paying you back for with this illness?"

I have put this as the tenth commandment because condemning your suffering friend is one of the worst things you can do. Please do not tell someone that if only she had more faith then her son would not have autism, her husband would find a job, or her cancer would be healed. The truth is, you have no idea what God is doing behind the scenes of your friend's suffering. If she is a believer, then Scripture says that all things work together for her good and God's glory (Rom. 8:28), but you don't know the intricate details of God's plans. In Genesis 3 we see that suffering occurs as a result of living in a fallen world. Elsewhere in the Bible we see that suffering can sometimes be the result of one's own sin (see Galatians 6). Furthermore, when Jesus heals a man born blind, he reveals another reason for suffering: "As he passed by, he saw a man blind from birth. And his disciples asked him, 'Rabbi, who sinned, this man or his parents, that he was born blind?' Jesus answered, 'It was not that this man sinned, or his parents, but that the works of God might be displayed in him'" (John 9:1–3). God allows suffering to show his great glory. To say that you know God is punishing your friend is just plain mean. It's yet another way that we try to "play God." If you see areas in someone's life that she needs to clean up, by all means encourage her to do so. But you are no better than Job's friends if you tell her that all her suffering is the result of something sinful she has done.

Instead of taking the place of God and condemning someone without knowing what's really happening, spend more time seeking to understand how that person is doing spiritually. Tell him, "I'm sorry, I have no idea why these things are happening to you." And then listen to see what is going on in his heart. You might help the person explore his spiritual health and not start with the assumption that his sin has brought about certain consequences. Brokenness in this world is not always (or even often) a direct result of that one individual's sin. We live in a fallen world, and there will be death and suffering regardless of how we live.

Putting It All Together

I recently received an email from someone who watched a video I made with a couple of other pastors on what not to say to someone suffering, and she sent me an email of encouragement. I think it brings together the things that I've talked about in this chapter.

Good morning,

I watched your video this morning on the above topic and I left a few comments. I still felt led to reach out to you to thank you personally for that video. As a person in ministry who went through traumatic loss (since 2010) and now being on the other side of that loss, still in recovery mode, I could really appreciate the dialogue that you and the other leaders shared.

I lost my mom in 2006, my dad in 2007 (11 months later), and people with good intentions felt the need to say something. The only problem was it was usually the wrong thing. Those examples that you all gave in the video are so true to life. When I lost my parents, they told me, "They're better off in glory." Well, what does that say for me, down here? Am I better off, LOL?

Then I lost my job in 2010, my home, possessions, and livelihood the same year. None of the people I thought would step up (Christians) did, but I did hear, "I'm going to be praying for you." My family was hungry, and while some helped, there were a lot more days we were hungry than not. People would say, "You're still looking for a job?" "Have you done inventory to see if your suffering is tied to something you have done? Maybe your children did something that caused this to happen to you?" Or the myriad of comments regarding confessing my sins and the suffering will be over. . . .

I believe God does not waste anything we go through, and I believe I will be able to help a lot of people, but sometimes, no words, just a hug, or no words, just a meal, or no words, just a smile will do.

Thank you for being living water to my soul and spirit today through your simple dialogue. I always say, "I know what NOT to say, and I have a deeper compassion for those suffering alone."

God bless all that you do.

I think that email sums this chapter up well. Whatever you do, don't do the things I've mentioned here! Make it your aim to love the hurting in a way that honors God and blesses your friend. Just like the story of the pilots who landed at the wrong airport, it doesn't matter how honest and noble your intentions are in helping the hurting if you hurt them even more. If you take the wrong approach to helping, you may have a rocky landing.

9

The Church's Gracious
Pursuit of the Hurting

I was on a student ministry trip with my church when I got the news. My team had been working on construction projects in Atlanta during our days, and our nights were filled with preaching and teaching in various churches. One evening we learned that another team's coleader had been hurt. I knew the student well, admired her, and had built a friendship with her. I didn't know it at the time, but she was my future wife!

The news about Gloria was not good. She had suffered a terrible injury after a nail was mishit by an experienced carpenter on their construction site. The nail flew across the site and struck her right eye, leaving her in shock and passed out on the ground. I'll spare you all the gruesome details, but her eye was deflated by the nail, and all the local doctor could do was sew her eye shut and refer her to a retina specialist. While it was a horrible accident, one of my favorite pictures is of Gloria with her eye bandaged shut eating a piece of pizza in the emergency room with a smile on her face.

In an act of providence, the doctor "happened" to have a friend who was known as *the* retina specialist of the southern United States. The specialist was in Dallas, just forty-five minutes away from Gloria's home. In another act of God's sovereignty, I was asked to help Gloria get to her doctor's appointments. When my wife and I tell others how our relationship began, we often say I fell in love with Gloria "when she had only one eye." It's the truth. Her right eye was almost a lost cause. Gloria's case was bleak, and the doctor had her pick out a glass eye he would put in if the surgery failed. It was a faint reality the doctor was preparing her for. Praise the Lord, a couple of months after the accident she had that major surgery, and her eye was saved. It wasn't completely healed, but she was able to keep her eye, and she can see fairly well with a contact lens. While I fell in love with the young woman "who had only one eye," I ended up marrying the woman with two eyes a little over a year later.

But even though the surgery was a miracle in itself, it wasn't the most miraculous thing I witnessed in those trying months.

The Most Miraculous Thing

While the medical care was incredible, and Gloria was able to keep her eye, the most miraculous thing was watching the church care for her during this trial. Our church rose to the occasion in ways that I had never seen before. Two men in our university student ministry appointed themselves to be stewards over all the volunteers who wanted to help Gloria. They spent time with her to find out what her needs really were, and they organized all offers of help before they got to her. This helped her not to be put on the spot with having to answer yes or no regarding whether she needed help, and it allowed her to receive the help she really needed. These men graciously operated as command central for our church's effort in caring for her.

After consulting with Gloria, these men assigned tasks to people, who would then bring help that she actually needed, not merely what they wanted to do. For example, when she needed car rides everywhere because her depth perception was gone, they found drivers. When they found out she couldn't walk up the steps to her classes, they found people to help her get to class on time. When she needed eye drops put in her eyes every few hours, different people were slotted to drop them in. Others did chores at her house and helped her at her nannying job. People even read her assignments to her because it put too much strain on her good eye to read for herself. Others came over to read the Bible to her. A rumor even got out that she loved coffee ice cream, and soon her freezer was filled with the stuff. (The only problem was that while she loved coffee and ice cream, she didn't care for coffee ice cream. But it was certainly a thoughtful gesture!)

The church also organized prayer for Gloria at their monthly prayer meeting. Our pastor Tommy shared the details of the injury with the church and led us in prayer for Gloria. Prayer requests were spread throughout our university ministry and regular updates were sent out to everyone. People from the church would often come over to her house to pray for her. Some would even call her to check in and pray for her right then on the call. Others would sit by her and be a friendly presence as she dealt with her new reality of potentially losing her eye.

The church did an outstanding job of caring for Gloria in her disability and pain. I got to see firsthand how beautiful it is when the church comes together and helps the hurting. Through the encouragement of others, Gloria's faith was strengthened. She felt supported in every way, and was able to witness to many people about the love of Christ when they asked about the pirate patch on her eye!

Nature of the Church

The word for *church* in the New Testament is used to describe both the visible and invisible church. In other words, it can refer to a local congregation or all Christians throughout the world and in all times. In his excellent book, *The Church*, Mark Dever notes that the actual word that we translate as "church" is the word *ekklesia* and is found 114 times in the New Testament. It literally means an "assembly." It is used three times in Acts 19 to describe the riot that is gathered in an amphitheater in Ephesus to deal with Paul, and two other times it simply describes an assembly. The other 109 times it describes a distinctly Christian assembly.[1] Scripture is clear that the church has visible form and is organized on earth as an observable society. Titus, 1 Timothy, and the early church in Acts tell us that it has members and leaders; it has biblical preaching; it has the ordinances of baptism and the Lord's Supper; it does church discipline and has clear order and priorities. The nature of the church is the local gathering of believers that marks off which people on earth are devoted to God. Dever argues that the mission of this local assembly is to be a corporate display of God's glory to the world. It is to spread forth the glory of Jesus Christ, our Savior.[2]

The Bible uses many different metaphors to describe what the church looks like. One of Paul's favorite analogies is that the church is a body (1 Cor. 12:12–20). He talks about how eyes need hands that need feet that need everything else. Paul's point is that no individual part of the body is more important than any other. We need eyes, and we need feet. Body parts do different things, but all are necessary. When one part of your body hurts, it's a distraction to you no matter which part it is. If your toenail is broken or your tooth is chipped, that could be the end of your day. You can't stop thinking about your tooth pain! This is the same for us in the church. When one part of the body of Christ is hurt, then it affects all of us because together we are in Christ.

Our community with one another exists only because of what Jesus Christ has done for each one of us. Therefore, care and concern should mark the body of Christ as a community. Author Thom Rainer puts it well in his book on church membership: "God did not give us local churches to become country clubs where membership means we have privileges and perks. He placed us in churches to serve, to care for others, to pray for leaders, to learn, to teach, to give, and, in some cases, to die for the sake of the gospel."[3] Later in the book Rainer adds,

> With a country club membership you pay others to do the work for you. With church membership, everyone has a role or function. That is why some are hands, feet, ears, or eyes. We are all different, but we are necessary parts of the whole. Each part, therefore, has to do its work, or the whole body suffers. There is a beautiful diversity in the midst of unity in church membership. The Bible makes it clear that if one part does not do its job, the whole body does not function well. But if one part does its job well, the whole body rejoices and is stronger.[4]

To be in a church is to consider others as more important than yourself. The Bible is ripe with exhortation to place others' interests over our own.

> So if there is any encouragement in Christ, any comfort from love, any participation in the Spirit, any affection and sympathy, complete my joy by being of the same mind, having the same love, being in full accord and of one mind. Do nothing from selfish ambition or conceit, but in humility count others more significant than yourselves. Let each of you look not only to his own interests, but also to the interests of others. (Phil. 2:1–4)

> And let us consider how to stir up one another to love and good works, not neglecting to meet together, as is the habit of some, but encouraging one another, and all the more as you see the Day drawing near. (Heb. 10:24–25)

The church should be the model of how a group cares for the hurting. Humility and selflessness should mark us just like it marked the church that helped Gloria when she injured her eye.

Bear One Another's Burdens

In a fallen world, it is inevitable that there will be times when a part of the body of Christ will be hurting. Galatians 6:2 gives us direction when this happens: "Bear one another's burdens, and so fulfill the law of Christ." The word for *burden* here is the word used to mean "a heavy weight or stone" someone is required to carry for a long distance.[5] The same English word *bear* is used later in Galatians 6:5: "For each will have to bear his own load." At first, verse 5 seems to contradict verse 2. We are told that we are to both carry each other's burdens *and* carry our own load. However, Paul makes a distinction. The word for *load* in verse 5 refers to a man's traveling pack, like a backpack.[6] When the Scripture says everyone must carry his own *weight* or *load*, it has in mind the weight of our personal responsibility before God. You will have to answer for what you do with what you've been given. This means you are responsible to disciple your kids, to work hard at your job, to walk with God. I can't do those things for you. You have to do them yourself.

But carrying another's *burden* is something different. Imagine somebody struggling underneath a huge crushing weight. How do you help him bear that burden? You almost have to get in his shoes. In order to carry the weight, you must come up right beside the person and relieve some of the weight he's carrying. This isn't easy work; it's going to cost you something. You will suffer when you bear someone's burdens. You might even experience drastic pain in helping him. This is what we see with Jesus.

In fact, the Bible frequently speaks of "bearing." It's even said that the whole work of Jesus Christ could be described in that one word.[7] Jesus has borne our griefs and carried our sorrows, and now the Christian is to bear that same cross. We bear one another's burdens in the church because Christ bore our burdens. When we say that we can't afford the money or the time to help someone, what we mean is that we don't want any of that person's trial to interfere with our lives. We're not living in light of Jesus as our burden-bearer. If you're not willing to see yourself burdened by others, you haven't fully understood Christ as the one who bore your burdens on the cross.

All too often we just want to help with what we can easily give up—a little money here, a little time there. At the end of the day, all we've really done is made ourselves feel better, haven't we? We've done our good Samaritan deed for the day or the week, and we feel okay. For many of us, it's easier to write out a check for a starving child halfway around the world than to share the burden of our neighbor who talks too much or irritates us. That distant child makes a slight dent in my checkbook, but my fellow church member interferes with my sleep, my time, my routines, and my calendar. If we think we love someone on the other side of the world but we can't be bothered by the image bearers right in front of us, we're deluding ourselves.

But You Can't Be the Savior

The apostle Paul is quite balanced when he challenges us in Galatians 6 to "carry one another's burdens." That charge implies that while we are to help people sacrificially, we don't drown ourselves in the process. It presupposes that by God's grace you can actually carry the burden someone is facing. You can't let it crush you. You shouldn't take out an outrageous, unpayable loan to help someone financially and fail to feed your family. You can't allow yourself to feel so responsible for someone's emotional or spiritual state that it paralyzes you, and you become so distracted and hurt by it that you can't function. If you pridefully take undue responsibility or feel guilted into taking undue responsibility, you are carrying something you are not meant to carry.

When you are doing such things, you're not really helping the other person. You might be enabling him or even using him to prove to yourself or others that you are worthwhile. You could be trying to atone for your own failings. Even more, you may be in the way of others who are equipped by God to bear that burden. That's why the church exists and why Paul calls it the body of Christ. Together the church is to care for one another, and so you are not alone in caring for the hurting.

Remember that Christ was ultimately the only one who was crushed by our burdens. And not just our burdens, but also our sin. All of it was on him. He was crushed for our iniquities. He is close to the brokenhearted and saves those crushed in spirit. He carries our sorrows and was pierced for our transgressions, and by his wounds we are healed. Don't try to be someone's savior, because it will crush you, and you will fail. People don't need you; they need Jesus.

A Culture of Care

Consider these profound words: "The church isn't a gas station (where your needs are met), but it's the bus that I'm supposed to be traveling on with other believers."[8] The church isn't a place you swing by for a quick fill-up and then go on your way. The journey of the Christian life is supposed to be made together with other believers on the same trip to the same destination.

We should always be looking out for needs in the church. As we consider a culture of care, an important question we should ask ourselves is, If everyone in our church served like me, what would our church look like? Would that be a good thing or not? Would our church look like a battleship getting ready for battle, with everyone working hard for the mission? Or would the church look more like a cruise ship, with everyone waiting for someone else to serve them?

One practical thing we can do is to be ready to serve on the mornings we head out to our corporate worship gatherings. We should go into the gathering with the mentality that we are ready to serve and help. We go into conversations asking intentional questions and greeting new people who come through the door. We like to joke at Redeemer Church of Dubai that each member is on the "unofficial connections team" that morning. This means we all have our radar antennas up looking for someone who is new or anyone who might have a need.

I love hearing about church members who initiate care for the hurting on their own. I recently heard from a member in our church who was very sick in the hospital, which left her husband and their four children both worried and struggling with his busy work schedule. It was a distressing two weeks for them, but it was incredibly encouraging when I later spoke with Rachel. She told me that the community of church members in their neighborhood went above and beyond in caring for their family during this difficult time. Families brought over meals and watched the children. The most encouraging thing to me is that it wasn't once brought to the elders' attention to organize something, but everything was taken care of by the members themselves.

The Second Most Important Book in the Church

Another way we can care for those hurting in the church is to know who our fellow members are in the first place. Garrett Kell calls the church's membership directory the second most important book in the church, after the Bible.[9] I think he's on to something. He means that as church members, we have a responsibility to know who the other members are. By having a picture directory at your disposal, you can easily learn the names of the members in the church. Building community as a church is easier when you have members who know each other's names and can therefore more easily initiate conversations together.

We should also take time regularly to pray for the members of the church. We encourage the members at Redeemer to keep the directory close to their Bibles so that they can use part of their devotional time each day to pray for one another. Our directory is around thirty pages long, and so we could take one page a day along with the Scripture we've just read and use that as ammunition for praying for our fellow members. This way you could legitimately pray for all the members of the church in a month. We also do this once a week as a staff team and follow it up with an email to those members letting them know we've prayed for them.

A third initiative is to think about ways that you can serve those individuals you just prayed for. By regularly looking through the pages of the church's directory, you can be easily reminded of the rest of your local body and what trials they might be dealing with. Perhaps a quick phone call of encouragement every once in a while is in order. In the back of our directory, we list all the members' birthdays. One of our elders, Frank, has made it a tradition to call the men in our church on their birthday and to pray for them on the phone. His wife, Sneha, calls the female members on their birthdays, and over the course of the year they prayed with each member of our church. What an encouragement they are as they shine the spotlight on Jesus in their care for the church.

A Word to Church Leaders

Church leaders can do many things to bless those who are hurting. It's important that elders show genuine concern for people who are suffering by contacting them and praying for them. As I mentioned, I've learned the hard way by failing to do so quickly enough and have hurt some in our congregation by not being responsive. It's also helpful for elders to communicate with one another so all of them know which sheep are hurting and need care. Having some practice in place to relay information is important. Perhaps even installing a diaconal ministry of member care could aid the elders and other members in caring for the hurting.

However, I have found that the most important thing that a pastor can do for the hurting sheep is to consistently preach the gospel to the congregation. The regular ministry of the Word is like a gas station and oil change center—it fuels and maintains your vehicle.[10] The church doesn't fundamentally need an exhortation to try harder, but it needs the truth that Jesus has already saved them. This helps to prepare church members for the inevitable suffering that will come to their lives and to the lives of those around them, and best speaks to the hearts of sufferers in their pain. As mentioned earlier in the book, there is nothing more important that people need to hear than the good news of Jesus Christ's death on the cross and his resurrection from the dead. It is imperative that pastors hold out this good news to their congregations every week. Paul considered this his life goal and aim when he wrote in Acts 20:24, "But I do not account my life of any value nor as precious to myself, if only I may finish my course and the ministry that I received from the Lord Jesus, to testify to the gospel of the grace of God."

As a church leader, it must be your aim and goal to see that the preaching, teaching, and ministry of your church is centered on Christ's finished work. Otherwise you will be leading souls on a weary journey of legalism and works that will only lead them to ruin. Point them to Christ, and let their weary souls be nurtured and find rest in him.

If you're a church member, you need to be involved in a church where the gospel is regularly preached and lived out. When the preaching of the gospel matches the church's glorious pursuit of the hurting, the beauty of the good news of Jesus is on full display for the world to see. May our churches be places of refuge for the hurting where they can be replenished by the love of Christ displayed through the people of God.

Conclusion

I'm sitting thirty-five thousand feet up in the air right now next to my two daughters, who are watching a movie. We've just left Dubai on a trip halfway around the world to the United States. It's always an adventure occupying two rows of seats and commencing twenty-four hours of travel with four children eight and under. It's a full-time job to keep the children from changing their movies one hundred times and angering the people sitting in front of them by tapping their screens continuously. And it takes karate skills to corral their legs from kicking the seat in front of them in their sleep or to keep them from falling off their own seat while they're sleeping. This particular trip was no different as we went through the gruesome experience of having one of our daughters throw up on everything a couple of times and another daughter losing her favorite teddy bear (the airline is still looking for lost Beary the Bear).

Flying around the world with our children is not usually the time to "get things done," but I still made ambitious plans to write the conclusion to this book on this flight. As I write, I'm still thinking about a traumatic experience I just had at the airport food court. We arrived at a restaurant for our preflight tradition of ice cream sundaes when a man walked out of another line and struck my elbow with his food tray as hard as I've been struck since I began to suffer from nerve pain. There I was with two ice creams in hand letting out a scream in the middle of the airport (thankfully no officials whisked me away). The tray had struck the mangled nerve in my arm, setting off fiery lightning pain throughout my body. In those times it's virtually impossible for me to hide or mask my reaction. Right there in the middle of the airport food court, with my two precious daughters by my side, I hunched over, screamed and couldn't move. The man felt bad, and I felt bad for him, but I turned down his request to help me carry the ice cream and I led my daughters back to our table.

I then left my family there to enjoy the ice cream and found a place to sit, alone. After the pain calmed down a bit and I was able to think more clearly, I processed what had happened. I was sad that my ailment wasn't healed. I realized that I would now have intense pain for the duration of our travels. I was angry. Whenever my pain is set off, there is also the fear that it will never calm down, and I'll never be healed. And maybe worst of all, I know that my girls were both shaken at seeing me in pain and reacting like I did. They were part sad, part embarrassed, and part helpless. I was so discouraged.

So now, how to end this book? I've just spent thousands of words on how to help someone in my situation. And here I am again. Discouraged and depressed. What do I need? How does my wife help me? And what about your friend? How do you care for your friend in chronic pain? How do you support the brokenhearted when they are in moments of despair over and over again? How do you love your friend dying of cancer? How can you make sure you'll love the hurting perfectly? I hope it is clear after reading all of these chapters that everything depends on the grace of God. And none of us loves perfectly except for Jesus. I hope you're not disappointed after reading this book to discover that I don't have the perfect equation for loving the hurting. There's no recipe you can follow that will give you the finished product in the precise way you'd like. This side of heaven there will be pain and sorrow, and we will at times be helpful and at other times we will be hurtful. Only Jesus perfectly loves the hurting.

Though there isn't a checklist of what you should do next, I pray that this book has helped you grieve your own loss in another's pain. And that you see how your walk with God has great bearing on your ministry to help others in their pain. I hope this book has given you some practical insight and advice on how to care for the suffering when you're not sure what to do.

But my greatest prayer is that this book has shown you that your only hope is found in the permanent circumstance of the gospel. That in the reality of Christ's birth, life, death, and resurrection, you can find meaning and significance for your life. That in the gospel you have found life and continue to find strength for loving those who are hurting.

Afterword

A Letter from My Wife

This week I (Gloria) received this goofy text message from my husband:

"I'm still locked in the bathroom. Haha! #Youhadonejob."

We were visiting with our friends Ronnie and Jenny in their home. Dave had asked me to come open the bathroom door for him in a couple minutes because he wouldn't be able to turn the door handle to get out. Meanwhile, I got carried away in conversation, catching up with our friends whom we hadn't seen in a long time. After several minutes of waiting for me, my poor husband began sending me text messages from inside the bathroom. When I finally remembered that I had one job (to help Dave open the door), I looked down at my phone and noticed his texts. Oops! This kind of thing happens to us all the time, and I'm glad we laughed about the incident instead of letting it turn into a conflict.

It feels surreal to be writing this chapter right now because Dave's chronic pain started exactly ten years ago this month. He came home from the Gospel of John class in seminary and told me that his pinky finger was buzzing. From that point on, his pain only grew and spread from one little finger to both of his hands and arms.

As dark as the days and nights have been at times, I'm overwhelmed by the grace we've tasted and seen in these ten years.

Friend, I'm so glad you've read this deeply personal and powerfully pastoral book. I wish I had a resource like this ten years ago when my otherwise healthy husband suddenly became disabled and depressed. Instead of immediately turning to God's Word for hope, I began taste-testing all the fake hope that is out there—hoping in man's opinions, medical miracles, and even thinking about the situation with an unchristian, karmaic rationale. I wonder if you've been down that avenue, too. There are fake hope vendors on both sides, hawking their wares and selling their false assurances.

Perhaps the biggest obstacle that prevented me from seeking real hope was that deep down I believed that our biggest problem was that Dave wasn't healthy. Both of us played the "if only" game, where you say things like, "If only we didn't have this health issue, then . . ." I don't know how many rounds of "if only" we played, but I do know it only ended in discouragement and distraction. Now, ten years later, sometimes I wonder if those dark days and nights would have been different "if only" we had fled to the cross immediately. Do you wonder things like that sometimes, too? The gospel trumps our regrets, and the grace of God prevails. On Christ is where we must fix our eyes when we think of the past, the present, and the future. As you've just read in these pages Jesus is the only true hope for us and our loved ones.

Meeting the Deepest Need

I know it is easy to look at someone who requires your help and to see only their felt need. You may feel as though the resources your friend needs are physical and that his demands on you are physical (energy, time, money, etc.). But while you are tending to another's physical needs, you must remember to consider his unseen need. The importance of attending to this unseen need is more dire than any issue your friend is facing.[1] Fellow believers need their faith to be strengthened by grace, and our nonbelieving friends need to have that grace dawn on them for the first time.

Our physical abilities and resources are all different. What you might have to do in order to help your friend might be different from how I care for my children or serve my husband. Sometimes their neediness might be exacerbated by circumstances—a surgery, an anniversary, an accident. It is easier to focus on the physical needs in those desperate times, but by God's grace you have to remember there are spiritual issues in the midst of all this. The world isn't going to help you stay aware of these things. In fact, Satan's goal is to distract you and keep you from recognizing your need for God. He is hell-bent against your taking the gospel to those hurting in your life. Friend, you may think you are only refilling medication, filling out paperwork, or writing a note of encouragement, but this is a spiritual war.

As you've read in this book, a hurting person's deepest problem is the same as your deepest problem. We were all made for unbroken fellowship with God, but our sin separates us from him. Our deepest need is to be reconciled with God, and our only hope is Jesus and his cross. Holding the truth of the gospel in your mind, respond to God's call on your life to serve others in word *and* in deed with the strength that God supplies so that Christ gets the glory.

How Do You Do It?

I wonder if people ever give you sad looks and say things like, "I can't imagine. I couldn't do what you do." They're right. But the reason they can't do what you do is not because you have some kind of superhero powers of servanthood that they don't have. The difference between your ministry and theirs is not an issue of competency. The reason you can do what you do is because this is your stewardship of grace. God has set you apart according to his unsearchable wisdom. He is the one who gives you everything you need to do what he's called and gifted you to do. When others around you say, "I couldn't do what you do," they are simply commenting on this fact: God has called and gifted you. And the correlating truth is that *you* couldn't do what God has called and gifted *others* to do, either!

Peter writes:

> As each has received a gift, use it to serve one another, as good stewards of God's varied grace: whoever speaks, as one who speaks oracles of God; whoever serves, as one who serves by the strength that God supplies—in order that in everything God may be glorified through Jesus Christ. To him belong glory and dominion forever and ever. Amen. (1 Pet. 4:10–11)

In college I took several "spiritual gifts inventories." I answered the multiple choice questions trying to envision the best possible merger of the person I was and the person I wanted to be. No wonder I always liked the composite descriptions of the inventory results! While resources like these can be helpful, they're not Jesus. At no point in any self-discovery inventory, book, or class was I ever given the label as one with "the gift of service." But Jesus didn't care. When he called me to serve my disabled husband, he equipped me with whatever I needed to serve with the strength he supplied. And he was faithful to give me his varied grace again and again as we added four children to our family over time. Jesus is generous to give me *everything* I need to serve him in the good works he planned for me (Eph. 2:8–10).

The underlying question that observers are asking you is this: How does *he* do it? How does God call and equip you? How does his glory shine through your service? When you are asked the "how" question, whether or not the asker recognizes God as the source of your ministry, assure yourself with this truth: Since God called you to serve someone, he will give you everything you need so that he may be glorified through Jesus Christ. We serve with joy through the same means by which we were saved in the first place: by grace through faith. To him belong glory and dominion forever and ever. In all circumstances, in every dark valley, in every moment. No exceptions. Amen.

Grace for Ministry Superheroes

If I could sit down with you and say something to strengthen your faith (this chapter is probably the closest I'll get!), then I would remind you to cling to that real hope in the gospel, just like Dave wrote about in this book. I would also encourage you to resist the temptation to be a ministry superhero. Since you have been busy serving others, you probably have an idea of what I'm talking about. A ministry superhero is someone who serves selflessly, invites the compassion of others, and then rejects their help for the sake of pride. The so-called selfless servant is actually seeking ways to serve themselves. This is a great temptation of mine. This kind of mentality is a sad, sick cycle of grace-rejecting sin.

When you have experienced a genuine loss of any kind, yet you pretend you are fine, you are *not* minimizing your pain. You are minimizing the genuine hope in Christ that is available to you because of the cross. When we do this, we are like a semiconscious surgery patient who utters to the doctor who stands ready to restore his life, "Oh, I'm fine. Don't worry about me." Rejecting the idea of our own neediness is a rejection of the grace available to us.

What we need to reject is the ministry superhero mentality. As good as pride feels in the moment, it will ultimately lead to our own downfall. In order to reject this mentality, you have to see Jesus as more precious than your pride. If you are suffering with the suffering, don't pretend you're not in pain. Cling to Jesus, grieve with hope, and gladly accept the help he sends.

Grace for the Bystanders, the Gawkers, and the Sincere Helpers

Sometimes when our family is out in public we look silly (okay, a lot of times!). I clip the littlest kid into his car seat, then walk around the minivan to open the passenger door for my husband. Then I clip him into his seat, too, careful not to graze his arms with the seatbelt. Then I close all the doors and hop in the driver's seat. It can take several minutes for this whole process, depending on how much stuff and how many people I need to load or unload into or out of the vehicle. We repeat the process in reverse when we arrive at our destination. If a passerby notices our family circus in a parking lot, they sometimes stare. And why wouldn't they? This week one couple actually stopped on the sidewalk in front of a gas station to watch. The unique work you do in caring for the hurting people in your life may or may not draw a crowd of onlookers or elicit the question-askers. But regardless of whether we wish we had more or less attention from others, we all need to remember to extend grace to the people around us (*and* those whom we wish were around us to help).

People stare. They avoid you. They follow you. They don't say anything. They say hurtful things. They don't try to help. They try to "help" (bless their hearts). Friends, even in our right evaluation of Job's friends and their reckless words, we need to take off our own judge-y pants. We are all bumbling fools apart from the grace of Jesus. Give grace to people who will not help you and to people who say all the wrong things. I don't know how much time I have wasted pouting about people instead of praising God. I have critiqued the help that others have given me more than I have meditated on what Jesus has done for me. It holds true whether you want more help or wish people would leave you alone for a minute: "the Lord is near to the brokenhearted and saves the crushed in spirit" (Ps. 34:18).

Grace for the Long Haul

I remember one night when I was pregnant with our second child and ailing from morning sickness. (Why they call it "morning" sickness when the nausea can strike any time of day is beyond me!) We were living in a town in Oman at the time, in a place where a woman couldn't exactly run to a restaurant and pick up some take-out. And of course, my husband couldn't open the front gate, open the car door, turn the ignition, drive himself to a restaurant, and carry a bag of food to bring back for us. I was feeling absolutely wretched at the thought of cooking meat (or any food). It's hard to say what made me feel more nauseous that night—standing at the kitchen sink with a kilogram of raw chicken in my hands or the roots of bitterness that were choking my heart.

It's hard to see what God is doing in dark times. We take it by faith that God is using the pain in our lives to produce for us an eternal weight of glory beyond all comparison (2 Cor. 4:16–18). And so we look to that which is unseen; we see things through an eternal perspective. That's what the anonymous hymn writer explained with lyrical excellence in the beloved hymn, "How Firm a Foundation":

> When through the deep waters I call thee to go,
> The rivers of sorrow shall not overflow;
> For I will be with thee thy troubles to bless
> And sanctify to thee thy deepest distress.
>
> When through fiery trials thy pathway shall lie,
> My grace, all-sufficient, shall be thy supply.
> The flames shall not hurt thee; I only design
> Thy dross to consume and thy gold to refine.[2]

When you can't see what the Potter is making, you trust the Potter. He delights in his sovereign will, so we don't have to apologize for God or feel embarrassed or embittered about what he has designed. He loves us with an everlasting love and is willing to put us through trials in order to purify us for himself. So we do not lose heart. Time can pass and "life" can happen. Yet we do not lose heart. We are dying on the outside, all of us. But by the grace of God in Jesus Christ, our inner self really is being renewed day by day. It really, *really* is! And that is a tremendously encouraging thought. Grace happens because God has willed it so. Praise the Lord! None of us deserves the grace to lift our sights to things that are unseen. Friend, I pray that he gives you everything you need to do everything he has called you to do—so that God may be glorified through Jesus Christ.

Recommended Resources

Chapter 1: Grieving Your Loss in Another's Pain

Walking with God through Pain and Suffering by Timothy Keller. This thorough book asks important questions such as, Why is there suffering in the world? How do we respond when difficult circumstances confront us?

A Grace Disguised: How the Soul Grows through Loss by Jerry Sittser. In one fatal car accident Sittser lost three generations of his family: his mother, his wife, and his young daughter. This book discusses the sorrow one deals with in sickness or death.

Experiencing Grief by H. Norman Wright. This brief and helpful book offers guidance on how to process your grief.

Chapter 2: Walking with God

How People Change by Timothy S. Lane and Paul David Tripp. This is a great book that gets to the heart of one's *own* sin and helps you consider how to respond to *others'* sin. It deals with how to change the heart by looking at how we grow in Christ.

Words to Winners of Souls by Horatius Bonar. Written by a nineteenth-century Scottish Presbyterian to those in ministry, this book's main point is that if you're not "much with God" you can't be "much with others." It is highly relevant for those who seek to love those who are in pain.

Chapter 3: Faithful Friendship

Life Together by Dietrich Bonhoeffer. This is easily my favorite book on Christian community.

The Four Loves by C. S. Lewis. Lewis does a masterful job of talking about friendship. This is one of the most helpful words on the topic I've ever read.

True Friendship by Vaughn Roberts. In this short book, Roberts discusses friendship in six sections: Friendship is crucial, close, constant, candid, careful, and Christ-centered.

The Company We Keep: In Search of Biblical Friendship by Jonathan Holmes. This book is a helpful primer on the importance of having good friends in your life.

Chapter 4: Be a Hope Dealer

Gospel Primer for Christians: Learning to See the Glories of God's Love by Milton Vincent. Gloria and I had no idea that this book would impact our lives as much as it has when our friends Kevin and Katie handed it to us straight off their coffee table a few years ago. It's a short book, but it is filled with gospel truth for everyone, with valuable excerpts for those going through trials. It is a great primer on how to preach gospel truth to yourself and be encouraged with what God has already done in your life, what he is doing in your life, and the hope that we have in the future.

Note to Self: The Discipline of Preaching to Yourself by Joe Thorn. This book of letters or notes to yourself is full of reminders of God's grace in our lives. It's devotional in nature and is great fuel for finding our joy in Christ's finished work for us.

What Is the Gospel? by Greg Gilbert. This is the best book I know of that explains the content of the gospel over the course of the entire book. Gilbert breaks the gospel down into four bite-sized parts: God, man, Christ, and response. It explains that God is our holy and creator God, man has sinned against God and deserves death and judgment, God in his grace sent Christ to die for our sins, and we must respond in repentance and belief. We've passed out this book to almost everyone in our church membership, and it's been useful instruction for them in learning the contents of the gospel.

The Explicit Gospel by Matt Chandler. This book is a reminder that oftentimes the gospel is left out of our churches. Chandler breaks down the gospel "on the ground" in a four-part outline: God, man, Christ, response. And he breaks down the gospel "in the air" in another four-part outline: creation, fall, redemption, consummation.

The Gospel: How the Church Portrays the Beauty of Christ by Ray Ortlund. This book takes the contents of the gospel and shows how it is central to the life of the church. The gospel must shape everything we do. While not explicitly speaking to those who are hurting, the truths in this book certainly apply.

Chapter 5: Serve Like Jesus

On Being a Servant of God by Warren Wiersbe. This book speaks from Wiersbe's honest experience in serving others in Christian ministry.

Chapter 6: The Power of God in Prayer

A Praying Life: Connecting with God in a Distracting World by Paul E. Miller. This encouraging book challenges Christians to talk to God like the Father that he is.

Prayer: Experiencing Awe and Intimacy with God by Timothy Keller. This excellent book on prayer is divided into five sections: (1) desiring prayer, (2) understanding prayer, (3) learning prayer, (4) deepening prayer, and (5) doing prayer.

Chapter 7: Hope for the Hard Conversations

Speaking Truth in Love by David Powlison. This book examines the process by which one believer speaks truths, sometimes difficult ones, to another person in love. This is an invaluable resource for people who are helping the hurting.

Chapter 8: Whatever You Do, Don't Do These Things

Visit the Sick: Ministering God's Grace in Times of Illness by Brian Croft. This is an excellent short book on practical things one can do when ministering to the hurting.

Chapter 9: The Church's Gracious Pursuit of the Hurting

The Church by Edmund P. Clowney. This is one of the best and most thorough primers on the church.

The Compelling Community: Where God's Power Makes a Church Attractive by Mark Dever and Jamie Dunlop. This new book talks about how the power of the gospel brings God's people together in ways that transcend all boundaries.

The Life of God in the Soul of the Church: The Root and Fruit of Spiritual Fellowship by Thabiti Anyabwile. This is one of the best books on spiritual fellowship. It seeks to answer the question, How should the body of Christ love and care for one another? Anyabwile works hard to show that Christ-centered community is not about programs but about our shared life in Christ.

Notes

Introduction

1. John Calvin, *Institutes of the Christian Religion*, ed. John T. McNeill, trans. Ford Lewis Battles (Philadelphia: Westminster, 1960), 1.11.8.

Chapter 1: Grieving Your Loss in Another's Pain

1. Charles Spurgeon, *Lectures to My Students* (Grand Rapids, MI: Zondervan, 1979), 163.
2. Jerry Sittser, *A Grace Disguised: How the Soul Grows through Loss* (Grand Rapids, MI: Zondervan, 1996), 47.
3. H. Norman Wright, *Experiencing Grief* (Nashville: B&H, 2004), 9.
4. Psalms 39 and 88 do not contain hope within the psalms themselves and have no "hope-filled" endings that we see in other psalms.
5. Derek Kidner, *Psalms 73–150: An Introduction and Commentary*, Tyndale Old Testament Commentaries (Downers Grove, IL: InterVarsity Press, 1975), 348.
6. Ibid., 350.
7. Tim Keller, *Walking with God through Pain and Suffering* (New York: Dutton Adult, 2013), 248.
8. Ibid., 250.
9. Ibid.
10. Ibid. I am indebted to Tim Keller's *Walking with God in Pain and Suffering*, particularly chapter 12, "Weeping." He provides an excellent analysis of Psalm 88 and points the reader to the hope found in Jesus facing *present* darkness so that believers don't have to face *eternal* darkness.
11. Kidner, *Psalms 73–150*, 350–51.

Chapter 2: Walking with God

1. Thomas Chalmers, *The Expulsive Power of a New Affection* (Minneapolis: Curiosmith, 1855), 19.
2. John Blanchard, *Truth for Life* (West Sussex, UK: H. E. Walter, 1982), 239.
3. Horatius Bonar, *Words to Winners of Souls* (Phillipsburg, NJ: P&R, 1995), 44–46.

4. John Flavel, *Keeping the Heart: How to Maintain Your Love for God* (Ross-shire, Scotland: Christian Focus), 21–22.

Chapter 3: Faithful Friendship

1. E. B. Smick, "Job," in *1 & 2 Kings, 1 & 2 Chronicles, Ezra, Nehemiah, Esther, Job*, The Expositor's Bible Commentary, ed. F. E. Gaebelein, vol. 4 (Grand Rapids, MI: Zondervan, 1988), 887.
2. R. L. Alden, *Job*, The New American Commentary, vol. 11 (Nashville: B&H, 1993), 70.
3. Ibid.
4. Joseph Bayly, *The View from a Hearse* (Colorado Springs: Cook, 1969), 40–41.
5. Dietrich Bonhoeffer, *Life Together* (New York: Harper and Row), 17–20.
6. Thomas à Kempis, *Of the Imitation of Christ: Four Books* (London: Paternoster, 1903), 63.
7. Scoop Jackson, "Antoine Walker's Story," July 28, 2014, ESPN.com, http://espn.go.com/nba/story/_/id/11262284/antoine-walker-reframes-tale-woe-sessions-scoop.
8. John Flavel, *Keeping the Heart: How to Maintain Your Love for God* (Ross-shire, Scotland: Christian Focus), 85–86.
9. Timothy Keller, "Proverbs: Friendship" (sermon, New York City: Redeemer Presbyterian Church, 2005), Timothy Keller Sermon Archive.
10. Ibid.
11. Ibid. This last section on Jesus and friendship has been influenced greatly by Tim Keller, who has transformed my thinking on this subject. I first heard this material in a sermon from Keller in 2005 on friendship, and his specific comments and footprint are seen throughout these last paragraphs.

Chapter 4: Be a Hope Dealer

1. Dietrich Bonhoeffer, *Life Together* (New York: Harper and Row, 1954), 22.
2. Ibid., 22–25.
3. J. Gresham Machen, *Christian Faith in the Modern World* (Grand Rapids, MI: Eerdmans, 1978), 57.
4. Timothy Keller, *Galatians for You* (Epsom, UK: The Good Book Company, 2013), 9.
5. One of my favorite seminary professors, Jim Allman, would always say this in our classes.
6. John Flavel, *Keeping the Heart: How to Maintain Your Love for God* (Ross-shire, Scotland: Christian Focus), 103–4.
7. These gospel application points have been heavily influenced by the numerous books I've read by Tim Keller and the many hours of sermons I've listened to where Keller so aptly applies the gospel to difficulties in life.
8. Milton Vincent, *A Gospel Primer for Christians* (Bemidji, MN: Focus, 2008).

9. Lewis A. Drummond, *Spurgeon: Prince of Preachers* (Grand Rapids, MI: Kregel, 1992), 90.

Chapter 5: Serve Like Jesus

1. J. Dwight Pentecost, *The Words and Works of Jesus Christ* (Grand Rapids, MI: Zondervan, 2000), 427–29.
2. D. A. Carson, *The Gospel according to John*, The Pillar New Testament Commentary (Grand Rapids, MI: Eerdmans, 1991), 463.
3. Thomas à Kempis, *Of the Imitation of Christ: Four Books* (London: Paternoster, 1903), 94–95.
4. I adapted this illustration from a presentation I once saw the late Calvin Miller share at a preaching conference.
5. Adapted from questions in Donald S. Whitney, *Spiritual Disciplines within the Church: Participating Fully in the Body of Christ* (Chicago: Moody, 1996), 113–16.

Chapter 6: The Power of God in Prayer

1. Andrew Bonar, *Robert Murray M'Cheyne* (Edinburgh, Scotland: Banner of Truth, 1960), 179.
2. Dietrich Bonhoeffer, *Life Together* (New York: Harper and Row, 1954), 36–37.

Chapter 7: Hope for the Hard Conversations

1. Dietrich Bonhoeffer, *Life Together* (New York: Harper and Row, 1954), 107.
2. Ibid.
3. Deepak Reju and Jeremy Pierre, *The Pastor and Counseling: The Basics of Shepherding Members in Need* (Wheaton, IL: Crossway, 2015), 38–39.
4. Ibid., 40.
5. These questions and comments are taken from David Powlison, *Seeing with New Eyes: Counseling and the Human Condition through the Lens of Scripture* (Phillipsburg, NJ: P&R, 2003), 129–45.
6. Timothy Keller, *Galatians for You* (Epsom, UK: The Good Book Company, 2013), 167.
7. Tim Chester, *You Can Change: God's Transforming Power for Our Sinful Behavior and Negative Emotions* (Wheaton, IL: Crossway, 2010), 158.
8. Paul Tripp, "Your Walk with God Is a Community Project," http://www.paultripp.com/your-walk-with-god.

Chapter 8: Whatever You Do, Don't Do These Things

1. "Misidentified Lights Led Southwest Pilots to Wrong Missouri Airport," *Daily News* website, January 17, 2014, http://www.nydailynews.com/news/national/misidentified-lights-led-southwest-pilots-wrong-missouri-airport-article-1.1583575.
2. C. S. Lewis, *The Weight of Glory* (San Francisco: HarperOne, 2001), 45–46.
3. Peter T. O'Brien, *The Letter to the Ephesians*, The Pillar New Testament Commentary (Grand Rapids, MI: Eerdmans, 1999), 164–65.

4. Michael A. Mullett, *Martin Luther*, Routledge Historical Biographies (New York: Rutledge, 2015), 108.

5. My friend Sue Bohlin wrote an excellent blog post on this subject, which helped me think through this material, particularly what not to say to the hurting. A commenter relayed this particular story. "What Not to Say When Someone Is Grieving," *Engage* (blog), http://blogs.bible.org/engage /sue_bohlin/what_not_to_say_when_someone_is_grieving.

Chapter 9: The Church's Gracious Pursuit of the Hurting

1. Mark Dever, *The Church: The Gospel Made Visible* (Nashville: B&H, 2012), 7–8.

2. Ibid., 8.

3. Thom Rainer, *I Am a Church Member: Discovering the Attitude That Makes the Difference* (Nashville: B&H, 2013), 6.

4. Ibid., 12–13.

5. Timothy George, *Galatians*, The New American Commentary, vol. 30 (Nashville: B&H, 1994), 418.

6. John Stott, *The Message of Galatians: Only One Way*, The Bible Speaks Today (Downers Grove, IL: InterVarsity Press, 1986), 159–60.

7. Dietrich Bonhoeffer, *Life Together* (New York: Harper and Row, 1954), 101.

8. Joshua Harris, *Dug Down Deep* (Colorado Springs: Multnomah, 2011), 203.

9. Garrett Kell, "The Second-Most Important Book for Every Christian," The Gospel Coalition, July 2, 2014, http://www.thegospelcoalition.org/article /the-second-most-important-book-for-every-christian.

10. Deepak Reju and Jeremy Pierre, *The Pastor and Counseling: The Basics of Shepherding Members in Need* (Wheaton, IL: Crossway, 2015), 17.

Afterword: A Letter from My Wife

1. One can object by saying, "Wouldn't a starving child's greatest need be bread?" Of course, a person with true faith wouldn't say to an emaciated person, "Go in peace, be warmed and filled," yet leave them without what they need for their body (James 2:16).

2. From John Rippon's *A Selection of Hymns from the Best Authors*, 1787; attributed variously to John Keene, Kirkham, and John Keith.

General Index

salvation, 62–63, 67, 69, 89, 119
sin, 35–36, 64–65, 75–76, 99–110, 127
Sittser, Jerry, 24, 155
small group Bible study, 43
social anxiety, 22
spiritual disciplines, 41
spiritual gifts, 150
Spurgeon, Charles, 24
suffering
in brokenness, 127
with disability, 17, 75, 79, 116

finding comfort in, 114–16
as identity, 116–17
redemption from, 27–28

Thomas à Kempis, 75
Thorn, Joe, 156
Tripp, Paul David, 109, 155

Vincent, Milton, 68, 156

widows, 75
Wiersbe, Warren, 157
Wright, H. Norman, 24, 155

Scripture Index

Scripture Index